THE PURPOSE of TRIALS AND ADVERSITY

Anne Trippe

THE PURPOSE of TRIALS AND ADVERSITY

Anne Trippe

Copyright © 2016 by Anne Trippe

The Purpose of Trials and Adversity
by Anne Trippe

Printed in the United States of America.

ISBN 9781498481588

All rights reserved solely by the author. The author guarantees all contents are original and do not infringe upon the legal rights of any other person or work. No part of this publication may be reproduced, stored in a retrieval system or transmitted in any form or by any means – electronic, mechanical, photocopy, recording or any other – except for brief quotations in printed reviews, without the prior permission of the author. The views expressed in this book are not necessarily those of the publisher.

Scripture quotations taken from the *New American Standard Bible* (NASB). Copyright © 1960, 1962, 1963, 1968, 1971, 1972, 1973, by The Lockman Foundation. Used by permission. All rights reserved.

Scripture quotations taken from the
King James Version (KJV) – *public domain*

Scripture quotations taken from the English Standard Version (ESV). Copyright © 2001 by Crossway, a publishing ministry of Good News Publishers. Used by permission. All rights reserved.

www.xulonpress.com

Table of Contents

1 Hard Times. 15
2 Could It Really Be…? 21
3 A Side Trip 25
4 Have You Heard? 31
5 Hard Times. But *Why*? 39
6 The Way We Are 43
7 Being Preppers 47
8 Prepped and Ready 53
9 The Attitude of Christ 59
10 The Baggage 63
11 Leave The Baggage 67
12 But How Is It Done?? 73
13 God's Awesome Purposes 81
14 Enter In and Partake 87
15 Is There A Line? 93
16 Do We Often Create Our Hard Times? 99
17 In Summary 109

Appendix 115

Foreword

God wants to use the trials and adversity you are facing right now to advance your spiritual growth and your enjoying God's best. God could remove all our trials from our lives with a word, but experience tells us He has chosen not to do that. Far more important than our ease, comfort, and pleasure is our spiritual growth. I know of several people who are mad at God because of the trials that have come their way. Until we are committed to the process of spiritual maturity, we will never understand the purpose of trials. In the book of James it says, "Consider it all joy, my brethren, when you encounter various trials, knowing that the testing of your faith produces endurance. And let endurance have its perfect result, that you may be perfect and complete, lacking in nothing." James 1:2-4

In her new book, Anne Trippe has done a remarkable job in clarifying the purpose of trials and the prepping it takes to endure when trials come. I encourage anyone reading this book to realize that the purpose of trials and adversity is God's most effective tool for spiritual growth. The degree to which we desire to grow spiritually and partake more fully of His promises, corresponds to the way we face the trials that come our way.

Dr. Charles Stanley
Senior Pastor
First Baptist Church of Atlanta

My intention and prayer in writing *The Purpose of Trials and Adversity* is for believers to understand, and be encouraged in knowing, that God has awesome purposes in His allowing difficult times to come in our lives.

We are often devastated and confused by adversity. We don't know how to think or what to do when facing hard times that involve, for example, unfairness, injustice, loss, or being prevented from accomplishing goals.

This book provides God's answer of how we are to respond to trials in order to grow and experience His blessings that are already ours in Christ. It might be something we wouldn't expect. And it involves a paradox. It involves God's very calling for believers.

Anne Trippe

More books and resources by Anne Trippe:

Marriage! The Journey
Old Beliefs vs New Beliefs
A Model for Marriage Counseling
Understanding Your Journey to Freedom

Introduction

T*he Purpose of Trials and Adversity* evolved from my facilitating thousands of counseling sessions with those who were hurting and from personal experiences in my own life and relationships. It became evident that believers are often angry, discouraged and puzzled about why a good God who saved us by His Grace and promised good things, would allow hard, unfair and painful trials in our lives.

No one welcomes adversity, and almost all of us regard our joy and contentment to be dependent on our personal situations and what we, or others, do or don't do. Sometimes we consider ourselves to be victims of the hard times that come.

Our search for lasting fulfillment and peace can be ongoing. But it seems that our circumstances block us from finding it. We run on empty much of the time, confused and wondering *why*.

We can feel hopeless, helpless, and without power to personally overcome the devastating times. Frequently, without being aware of it, discouraged individuals walk by self-imposed rules and self-defeating beliefs, which lead to feelings as guilt, rejection, inferiority, anger, depression or fear as they face the difficulties of life.

We need to learn to trust God and be *prepared in advance* to respond in faith when a crisis comes and we are devastated. If we aren't equipped with truth, we can feel defeated and fearful. It is usually very hard to *begin* learning truth when we are in the middle of a hard trial.

The truths on the following pages can help believers understand God's purpose in allowing them to walk through adversity. My desire is for them to see that since they, by God's grace, are new creations having been set free from being bound, it is possible to be prepared to live and respond to hard times out of Christ's life and power which indwells them. In doing so, they can *enter into the experience* of His freedom, peace, power, and sufficiency that is already theirs in Him.

When facing trials and hard times, the problem and the solution each might include things we wouldn't suspect. The chapters in this book will take us to places we might not have considered. Would you believe that scripture actually encourages us to be "preppers"– to get ready for the trials that will come? But in the book, before we learn to be "preppers", we take a side trip to unearth some origins and discover a mystery.

Did you know our learning to respond correctly to adversity includes what we call a "paradox", an enigma to the world system? And this paradox is a picture of God Himself? There is a chapter explaining the lines that must be drawn as this paradox is lived out. As readers progress through the book, they will learn what God's will is for them. They will see that His purposes are actually woven into and worked out of trials and adversities in the lives of His people–a divine design. Experiencing and exposing the Life that dwells in born-again believers is a main theme in the book.

1

Hard Times

They happen to everyone.
They are often unfair, unjust, unexpected.
Sometimes they are ordinary daily circumstances. Sometimes not.

Sometimes they are little. Sometimes they grow slowly. Some are fully developed. Sometimes they blind-side us. Sometimes they are like wild fires. Sometimes like continually smoldering embers. Some are like piercing thorns. Sometimes they can be tragic to us.

Because of them
Sometimes we crash and burn.
Sometimes we make it through with scars.
Sometimes we overcome them and grow.
Sometimes we get tough, and perhaps unapproachable.

Some of them *we* can cause – *or* not
By trying to get acceptance or respect from others.
By trying to protect ourselves and find a safe place.
By greed.

The Purpose of Trials and Adversity

By pride.
By having to win.
By trying to escape pain.
By trying to prove we are right.
By impatience.
By trying to find contentment in achievements, people, a place, or possessions.
By trying to get what we think we deserve and need by *our own ways that seem right and look good*.
By ways to get a high and avoid depression.
By our being in the wrong place at the wrong time.
By our doing what we shouldn't – OR not.
By being joined too closely with gossips or abusive people.
By making choices based on emotions.
By putting trust in people.
By dwelling on the past.
By blame and/or complaining.
By taking responsibility for others emotions and trying 'fix', protect, or to force good things to work out for others.

Most people are devastated and puzzled about why they are

Misunderstood	Abused
Lied about	Hacked
Criticized	Judged
Put down	Taken advantage of or swindled
Falsely accused	Blocked, hindered

They don't understand why hard times can involve
Feeling inadequate, rejected.
Not being able to please others.
Suffering injustices, retaliation.

Feeling without hope, contentment or joy.
Not being able to make it financially and emotionally in life.
Being insulted.
Not understanding why some have enough and some don't.
Others changing plans and creating confusion.
Others being demanding, inconsiderate of my schedule.
Ongoing inconveniences.
Significant others continually having opposite opinions.
Suffering harm because of others' mistakes.
Resistances / Irritations.
Plans and hopes dashed.
Physical and/or emotional suffering.
Various fears.
Losing loved ones by death, divorce, disability.
A loved one's addiction.
Being married to a narcissist.

Hard Times can also happen, for example, when

* Those with whom we are in various types of relationships–business or personal – repeatedly "tie knots differently than we do"– and it is hard to untie them.

* One person relies on order, planning and logistics and the partner or co-worker is the same, but with a *different* order. OR when the other partner is spontaneous, disorganized, doesn't plan.

* On a continuing basis, certain people communicate by assuming, interpreting, insinuating, and speaking indirectly, and are confused and / or threatened by people who are direct, and vice-versa.

A certain type of situation that is a hard time, a crisis, or a trial for one person may not be a trial for another person.

Trials *may not* be intentional...but sometimes they *are* on purpose.

In a trial, there may be a way that **seems right** to us–to our own understanding. Consequently, we can make plans and ask God to bless them. We may believe they are God's will, and we count on them happening. Then we are disappointed and confused to the utmost if they don't materialize as we envisioned. We can find ourselves in a hard time, a trial, and we may question God.

Maybe we didn't use Godly wisdom and prudence, because we believed that being practical isn't walking by faith. But then we find we must *get out* of the situation *by* the practical! In the world, we must adhere to certain principles in finances and to rules in other areas, or things do not work out for us. But hard times come to all people regardless. We must remember that when we make plans, they *will* likely change. There *will* be roadblocks and detours to our goals being accomplished. They *will* likely take more time, more effort and be more costly than we thought. We may face difficult times if we are non-committal and fear being specific when making plans and/or interacting with others.

For various reasons, we may be in a *fiery* trial and feel burned like we are in a *crucible*. And we ask ourselves what went wrong.

We may try to "fix" our Hard Times by

* Doing more of the same, yet continuing to get more of the same.
* Anger / Retaliation.
* Gossip.
* Trying harder to please / rescuing / enabling.

* Finding ways to escape, ignore, or avoid the problem.
* Becoming strong and kicking against the goads in other ways.
* Considering suicide.
* Praying the Lord would take away the adversity, heal us, and give us the things or people we believe we need.

And nothing changes.

We can become bitter, weary, exhausted, faint, defeated and maybe we 'give-up' and 'give-out'. And we trust our feelings as barometers of truth. In *Families Where Grace Is In Place*, Jeff Van Vonderan said we can become **T.I.R.E.D.** and **feel**

T = Trapped
I = Indicted
R = Responsible
E = Exposed
D = Defensive

Adversity in life isn't always our fault. But sometimes it is. When we put faith / hope in ourselves, in others or in our circumstances, we usually wind up angry and discouraged.

2

Could It Really Be..?

Several years ago I would often hear this old Irish Blessing:

> May the road rise up to meet you. May the winds be always at your back. May the sun shine warm upon your face. May the rains fall soft upon your fields.
> And until we meet again, may God hold you in the palm of His hand.

People tell me this Blessing is optimistic, positive, and comforting. And it is. However when I hear it, I am reminded that believers frequently see a path of ease, comfort, and freedom from painful circumstances with few obstacles in our way as God's will for us and the ultimate Christian life.

Therefore many claim God's promises, often with an emphasis on health, prosperity and financial success obtained by following certain kingdom principles or religious rules, and a relationship with God *may* be mentioned…or maybe not. And it isn't working.

I must be careful to explain that I believe it is appropriate and desirable for believers to speak positive acknowledgements based on the Truth of scripture, and to enjoy good health and prosperity–for soul and body. I also believe in meditating on the Scriptures and being in prayer, but these are not formulas nor religious "laws" we are to live by. Rather, they are endeavors for the purpose of instructing, helping and encouraging us in our Christian walk.

There are those in Christ who are praying "hedges of protection" in every valley so that "nothing shall by any means harm" them and so they won't "dash their foot against a stone". Instead, they experience calamities. And it isn't working. Others believe they must try to do everything perfectly according to religious "rules" to avoid pain and suffering. And it isn't working.

Hard times come to ALL regardless of the cause.

People often wonder why some Godly minister or other saintly person endures illness, persecution, or loss when it is evident that he/she has been dedicated to serving and knowing Christ. How many times have we heard these questions, "Why is this horrible thing happening to me? I've been close to God and am just as good as the next person. If God is a loving God, why would He allow such bad things to happen to me and my loved ones?"

Some of us, in an attempt to answer this for ourselves, will have intense guilt or resentment as we become introspective and focus on the past or on what we, or another person, did or did not do to bring about the adversity. On the other hand, religious people may say, "The devil is really after me," or "I guess I forgot to put my armor on this morning," or "maybe I should have fasted and prayed more," or "I exercised faith in God's grace and His protection, but the tornado hit us anyway." Or we might just become angry with God.

Could it really be....?

Trials and adversity come to all people, and scripture tells us these hard times happen to believers and non-believers alike. But we have difficulty understanding that injustice, unfairness, grief, and distress are allowed by God for a purpose, whether these things happen as a consequence of something we have done–or not. And it is hard to comprehend that God would orchestrate these difficult times together with all other circumstances in the lives of those who love Him so the result would be for their good and His glory. **Could this really be true?**

Could it be?

Could it be that we don't recognize the very tools the Lord would use to bring us into his best, to even conform us to His image? This is a huge matter for us to consider–and understand.

For a lot of us, adversity was involved in our first believing the truth and receiving Christ. But did you know that the Christian life is one where we can *expect* trials? Did you know it is by our accepting the trials and hard times with the right response that we can experience God's fulfillment and access the Grace and gifts that He has already given us – and that Christ will be revealed through us? **Could it really be…? Yes, it is true.**

A sweet young lady, who is a believer, said to me, "I have heard the message that believers can expect to have hard times and trials, but it makes me depressed to think about it…" She had not yet begun to realize that there is a way to face unfairness and adversity that could lead her to freedom from depression, and into other blessings she never expected.

And yes, there can be a "fine line" in accepting one's unfair circumstances and staying in ongoing abusive situations, which she had experienced. A friend of hers had once told her to just trust God, buck up and be courageous, because God was her healer. He IS our healer, our safety, and our sufficiency. And we can rest in that fact. But the first step in appropriating that truth is to first understand something of the problem.

To grasp it all, we will take a side trip to unearth some origins and discover a mystery. So hang in there.

3

A Side Trip:
Unearthing Origins & Discovering a Mystery

In order for us to comprehend

God's purpose in allowing the hard times, unfairness, crises and trials we experience, it can help for us to understand something about the problem and how it began. As born–again believers, we all deal with difficulties in our daily lives and relationships. We can wind up angry, disappointed, depressed, fearful, and unforgiving. And there is often confusion and misunderstanding regarding why we can't rise above our emotions and circumstances.

The source of our struggles could be something that we might not suspect. Believe it or not, if we travel back to the beginning, we can unearth the origins of our obstacles. We will get a glimpse of how our own ways, our beliefs and behaviors for living life and facing trials, were developed. While there, we can also learn how our ways are related to who we were before we received Christ and were born-again.

And then, we will uncover the solution–something that was hidden by God for thousands of years but has now been revealed. So we will begin a brief side trip to explore those origins *and* discover a mystery indeed.

Back to the Beginning

As you know, in the beginning of humanity God created Adam and Eve *in His likeness*. Genesis 1:26 He breathed His breath of life into them. Genesis 2:7, 5:1 The Hebrew word for spirit is *ruach*– the same word for *breath* and *life* and *spirit*. They had His life, and it was their source. So they knew God, fellowshipped with Him, and their needs were met by Him. They were accepted by God.

But then they sinned. They disobeyed God's one command to them. As a result, **they died.** Genesis 2:17 They did not die physically, but spiritually. The word 'death' means *separation* in the sense that they had no more connection with God and no longer experienced God's life dwelling in their human spirits.

They were separated from God's life and communion with Him. *Their spirits* **had died to God's life**. They were left depending only on their human life and *their own resources*. After their fall they were left empty, needy, destitute and no longer complete. They were in a crisis–a real crisis.

The result was that **all of mankind, all of us, inherited their sin and death**. Romans 5: 12, 18 All are born "in Adam"–dead in sin. Ephesians 2:1,4,5, 1 Corinthians 15:22, Romans 3:23 Thus all are separated from God's life and enslaved and bound by the power of sin, *which can either look bad OR good*. So from birth a *human's identity* is *sinner*.

Romans 6:6, 6:17, 5:8

After Adam and Eve sinned, they were filled with pride, control, guilt, and fear. Because of their emptiness and neediness, they were driven to try to get from their performance and from each other the things they had previously received so freely and unconditionally from God's life. They walked independently of God as they tried to regain what had been lost. The outcome was that they developed certain ways of thinking. These ways included *false beliefs* about God, about themselves, about how to face crises, fill emptiness, and meet needs of security, contentment and worth. *These were the origins of our ways.*

And so it is with us, their descendants. Since their nature of sin, death and neediness was inherited by all of us, and we were bound by it, we do just as they did. We also draw conclusions and develop certain beliefs and behavior patterns to manage life and try to meet our needs, fill our longings, be safe, and deal with trials and pain. It is all about us, *and our ways of coping can seem right*. But these ways bring frustration and emptiness, and any peace is elusive, temporary–especially in our hard times and crises. And even though we may seek to know the one true God, we cannot, because sin and death separate us from His life.

All of that is a **problem**......actually it was THE problem.

But God provided THE solution. He also revealed a truth that had been kept secret since the beginning, and what a mystery it was!

The Solution

In God's timing, and by His *unconditional* love, mercy and grace, He sent His Son, Jesus, to be the sacrifice for and pay the penalty for the sin by which we were bound. And Jesus abolished spiritual death that separated us from God and from knowing His comfort and peace. By Him, *believers* are born of His Spirit, and we are set free from the chains that enslaved us.

While we were enemies, God reconciled us to Himself. This means God made us at peace with Himself through the death of His Son. Much more, having been **reconciled,** we shall be *saved* by *His life*. Romans 5:10 Believers have been *justified* by Christ's death. Romans 3:24; 5:9,18; 6:6 This means that all guilt and punishment for my sin was removed. It means *we who were **dead in sin*** were ***made alive*** (born again) by His life in us and declared right before God. 1 Corinthians 15:22; Ephesians 2:4-5

By God's love, mercy and grace, we were acquitted of guilt (declared not guilty) and brought into His favor. God no longer holds *any* sin against those of us for whom Christ died and who have been born of His Spirit. We are forgiven of ALL of our sins– past, present and future. Colossians 2:13 AND our *old self* was actually crucified *with Him*, so that our body of **sin** might be done away with, and we **would no longer be slaves to sin.** Romans 6:6 This is an amazing truth.

A Mystery Revealed

God chose us from the beginning to believe the Truth and be born a second time – born of His Spirit. John. 3:5-8, 2 Thessalonians 2:13 *It is a spiritual birth, where God imparts His life / spirit to literally indwell our new spirit, making us **new creations** with a new nature and new identity.* **Since our spirit is our basic nature and identity, we are made** *holy, saints* **and the very** *righteousness of God* **in Christ, accepted in Him.** 2 Corinthians 5:17, 21; 6:15, Ephesians 1:6 (KJV)

When God's Spirit and Life comes to live in us, it *replaces* our old spirit that was dead to *(separated from)* His Life. We become joined with Him, one spirit with Him. 1 Corinthians 6:17 He *put His life* in our mortal bodies. Romans 8:11 Born again people become the temple of God. 1 Corinthians 3:16; 6:17,19. We are literally placed in Christ and He in us. Being in Christ, we have also been placed with Him in the Father. 1 Corinthians 1:30, John 14:20

As new creations, we have been set free from sin's power over us and are connected to God. We are literally in union with Christ. God gave us His Life–Christ's Life–to indwell our spirit, in exchange for the sin and death in us that inhabited our spirit and separated us from Him. He came to dwell in us and *become our life* – our power and sufficiency. He is *eternal life in us*. **And this is the mystery that was hidden from all the generations before Christ. It is, "Christ in you, the hope of glory."** Colossians 1:25-27; 3:4 Ephesians 3:9

His Life in us becomes our new SOURCE of power and provision. Our power for choosing to walk in, and experience, our new life is derived from Christ's Spirit in us. Galatians 2:20 says that I am crucified with Christ: nevertheless I live; yet not I, but Christ liveth in me: and the life which I now live in the flesh I live by the faith of the Son of God, who loved me, and gave himself for me. (KJV)

Believers may not *feel* all of this is true. But it is. Quite often someone will say the truths presented here are just "the way God sees us" and are not literal. There are many metaphors and allegories in scripture, but these are literal truths.

Knowing these truths and the mystery of Christ indwelling life and power is necessary for us to begin to comprehend the purpose in God allowing hard times in our lives.

4

Have You Heard?

When facing crises or hard times, we can face them with anger, fear, shame, self-condemnation, or confusion. But **have you heard** we don't have to face adversity this way? We who have received Christ, *may not have heard* about that mystery and how we have been set free from condemnation, spiritual death, and have become new creations with Christ actually living in us. Even though Christ is our new life, *we may not face our trials as though He is our life – our power source, our sufficiency, our comfort, our worth, and has already provided all we need.* So we live empty and *as if* we are still chained.

However, some of us *have heard* these truths and are *still* facing crises, hard times, and road-blocks with fear, shame, confusion and self-condemnation. We don't know how to live from the truth, so we still try to control life to meet needs and longings, and protect ourselves and those we love from despair and pain–by our same old patterns.

These old patterns of thinking and doing *might* be difficult to identify because they seem so normal and reasonable. They may even look good. So we continue to do what we think makes sense and live out of the defeating emotions–*our feelings*–that result from a wrong mind-set. *We believe that emotions represent truth.*

In other words

Once we are born-again, we *can* still think according to our "pre-salvation" state. We can think like we've always thought. We can make decisions based on the way we have always made decisions. We respond to people like we've always responded. And we can think of ourselves as we've always thought of ourselves.

We think if others would change, "do-right", or "get on track" (on my sensible agenda), then my life would be okay. If they don't, I live frustrated and fearful of what might happen.

We see no purpose in pain, loss or failure, and we try to avoid it at all costs. We believe we are designed to find comfort and fulfillment in people or performance or maybe possessions. We haven't yet learned to turn loose of our familiar ways and trust God for comfort and contentment. It is scary. And we just want relief.

Most of us believe that trusting God is things turning out like we want and believe we need. For most it is *not,* "If I trust God, I'll be fine regardless of the outcome." It isn't in our having the purpose of finding comfort in God and resting in Him to be enough for us. We don't understand that–or HOW to even believe it. Could it be that we haven't heard the Truth or haven't understood how to walk in it?

We *may* be in a trial or crisis and not even realize it – much less know God is allowing it for a purpose. And nothing brings relief. When we experience loss or emotional and physical suffering, some of our fears in these crises can be:

* Fear of things not working out the way I think they should for me and my loved ones to be okay.
* Fear of not knowing how to cope with the unknown.
* Fear and worry because I believe I need people and their approval to be okay and find comfort.
* Fear because I feel responsible for others' well-being, and fearing if I can't make them okay, they will live in despair.

We believers can just sit still and be devastated by fears and the hard times that come, or we can kick against them and nothing changes inside. We can continue approaching life out of old ingrained beliefs and attitudes and resist believing truths of God's goodness toward us. And nothing changes.

We can see the situation or the crisis itself as the source of our struggles. But the reason we can't get past the adversity is usually something we might not expect. It is the way we think–our mind-set. And it is what we believe, or do not believe, about God's love for us and how to live in it and from it.

When we live according to old false belief and behavior patterns, we live in the futility of our own minds (Ephesians 4:17), trusting our own ways rather than the truth of who we are as born-again believers and God's love, provision and protection for us. In order to enjoy and experience our new freedom, contentment and life in Christ as we face difficult times and adversity, we need to trust that He will sustain us emotionally and provide for us in every way even when we are gripped by fear, anger, sadness or feeling hopeless.

You may be wondering what I mean when I say believers can have "false beliefs and behavior patterns." So on following pages is a chart of some typical wrong beliefs and resulting behaviors that can *lo*ok good, be well-intentioned or even religious. Do you have any similar beliefs and behaviors? (These same beliefs can also result in "bad- looking" behaviors.)

Later we will see how our false beliefs are related to our trials.

After the chart is a page of scripture references to encourage you. It is titled, **"Truths of God's Love for Me"**.

Examples of False Beliefs and Behaviors

These are fleshly patterns that can look good, be well-intentioned or even religious.

Below are some learned beliefs and resulting behaviors that we develop to meet needs, face trials, and make life work the best way we know how. They may *seem right* and make sense. But they arise out of fear of rejection and emptiness, and lead to disappointment, defeat and fatigue. And any peace is temporary. The patterns are all about self, protecting ego, finding fulfillment, contentment and being safe. *(The way these beliefs are lived out can look good as described here. Or the resulting behaviors can look negative, abusive, demanding, critical, intolerant, and resentful.)*

False Beliefs	Possible Resulting Behaviors
I must please God and/or others to feel **I am accepted / worthy.**	Serving with the church and/or serving others. Giving. Being a nice "people-pleaser" in relationships. *Or* maybe rescuing or trying harder to fix others than the others try to help themselves.
I must be a moral person and follow religious laws **to be forgiven and accepted.**	Focused on putting away sinful behaviors; perhaps being "preachy". Clean living. Seems moral and nice. But privately failing. Attending religious activities.
I must succeed to **find fulfillment and know I am of worth.**	Being charming, dedicated, driven, successful and at the top. May help others to succeed.

I must be respected **to know I am of worth, significant.**	May be involved in causes that focus on securing a special acknowledgement for certain groups or individuals.
I must be in control **to be secure and have peace.**	This person may or may not be dominant. He/she may be quietly resistant. May be unassuming. May provide for the family. Nice to others.
I must do things perfectly **to find significance and be secure.**	Is a perfectionist.. Organized, orderly. Subtly controls life, others or groups to fit his/her order. Does logistics well.
I must achieve power and recognition and be on top **to know I am of value.**	Applying one's self, pushing forward. Is intelligent, steady, reciprocal, articulate.
What I do makes me **who I am.**	High achiever, cordial, maybe religious. Works at connecting with people. OR feeling hopeless because I can live up to certain standards.
I need relationships to be **secure and fulfilled.**	Is people-oriented, friendly and joins groups. May attend church.

In the Appendix of this book, the following resources can be tremendously helpful for believers to renew our minds to truth:

- A chart which lists some False Beliefs and contrasts them with Scriptural Truths from which we can learn to live.
- A page listing truths of "My True Identity In Christ".

Truths of God's Love for Me

Often we have wrong beliefs about God's Love. We can see Him as we see humans who have had either positive or negative influences in our lives. God's love is not a desire for something. God's love doesn't dismiss justice. His love is not selfish. It is not as human emotional love.

The following truths can help us see and receive God's Love.

Three aspects of **WHO God IS** – His nature.
1) "God IS Spirit" John 4:24
2) "God IS Light" I John 1:5
3) "God IS Love" I John 4:8,16

God LOVES me VOLUNTARILY & UNCONDITIONALLY.
His Love is not based on anything I do or do not do. It is rich in Mercy and full of Grace. He unconditionally accepts me. Romans 5:8, Ephesians 1:3-4, 2:4-5, 1 John 4:9-11.

God LOVES me SACRIFICIALLY. I John 4:9-10 One can sacrifice without loving. I Corinthians 13:3 But one cannot love without sacrificing. Christ's Love is sacrificial. John 15:13 God's sacrificial Love SERVES. Philippians 2: 5-8 God's sacrificial Love is UNDESERVED and UNCONDITIONAL. I John 4:10a; Romans 5:8 He gave Himself up for me. Galatians 2:20, Ephesians 5:2

God's LOVE HEALS me. He is Jehovah Rophi Exodus 15:26

God's LOVE PROVIDES for me. He is Jehovah-Jireh Genesis 22:11-14; 22:23

God's LOVE is the love of a Father who **PROTECTS me**. Psalm 91

God LOVES me the *SAME* as He loves Christ. John 17:23; 15:9.

God's LOVE for me is INFINITE. It is so staggering that it surpasses knowledge Ephesians 3:19 with power that is far beyond what we can ask or think. Ephesians 3:20 The depth of His care for us is unfathomable. Psalm 139

5

Hard Times. But *Why*?

Having learned something about the origins of our own ways of facing life and the mystery that God revealed of His love, grace, and Christ in us, we still ask, "But what is the reason for hard times, the trials and adversity we go through?" Is it really related in any way to our living life according to our own strategies (wrong thinking and the resulting behaviors that might look good *or* bad)? If so, *why*? **Could there be a "divine design" woven into it all?**

We don't easily turn loose of our familiar and often good-looking fleshly patterns. These are ways which *block* our *experience* of Christ's Life and freedom that dwells in us and the good gifts that *have already been given to us* as believers.

Now imagine this. We can be so attached to those self-centered ways that, in the grand scheme of life, God allows among other things, the unique personalities and the actions of *certain people to become some of the specific instruments He works together in an omniscient design to break our hold on our ineffective ways*! Their ways may be reciprocal to our ways. *And their ways can become our hard times.*

Other natural occurrences can also become the tools God uses in one's life. It might be illnesses, financial loss, death of a loved one, persecution and loss of reputation because of someone's jealousy, or even the consequences of one's own behavior. It might be an attack by the powers of darkness. There are a number of various adversities in life. They can be large or small afflictions of body or mind. But whatever hard time we encounter is perfectly suited to loosen our grip on specific areas of our living independently of God's power in us.

This speaks a bit of how God works *all things together* for good for those who love Him and are called according to His purpose. *And that purpose is to conform us to the imag*e of Christ. Romans 8:28-29 Okay. So God uses trials, crises, and adversity as opportunities for us to be broken of walking in ways that prevent us from experiencing His best for us. AND that isn't all.

There is more to know

In 1 Peter 4:12-17, believers are told **not to be surprised** that a fiery ordeal or hard time comes, as if some strange thing were happening to them, because *it's purpose is to test them*. The test is to *reveal who they are* and *if they are walking after the Spirit*.

2 Thessalonians 1:4-5 calls adversities and persecutions a clear indication of **the righteous judgment of God**. Here *judgment* means the trial is a test or process that *brings to light* whether believers will respond by walking by the Spirit and Truth OR if they will harden their heart, resist yielding to God, and willfully continue after the fleshly mind-set and behaviors.

The test or trial is a judgment in the sense that our response to **it can reveal Christ through us**, showing and proving that we have been born of God and made worthy by Him for His kingdom. Here, being worthy doesn't mean our earning or deserving to partake of the righteousness, joy, and peace of God's Kingdom.

Scripture tells us that trials and adversity will happen to **all** people.

They are a judgment of all, both those who are alive in Christ and those who are dead in sin. 1 Peter 5:9, 4:17 For believers, trials and hard times are *God's discipline and training in our lives to unveil Christ in us and bring us to a place of experiencing His Life and the promises He has already given us.* Hebrews 12:4-8, 1 Corinthians 11:32

6

The Way We Are

At this point you are probably ready for the answer to this question: "W*hat* does knowing we were born of Christ's Spirit and are new creations who might have a wrong belief system have to do with facing trials and adversity?" You are about to find out.

First we need to understand that when we live life out of our old thinking and strategies (which scripture calls *flesh* and which can seem okay), we aren't prepared to overcome the trials, crises and difficulties that life brings. So we need to understand a little more about how all of this works.

As already mentioned, while under the power of sin and death and before we know Truth, **we** *draw conclusions and develop certain beliefs* about how we can make life work for us – how we can manage to fill our emptiness, satisfy our neediness, and be safe. Our beliefs or thinking is formed in the context of families, church, media, culture, school and peers,

Our needs and longings can be put under three categories – **security, worth** and **contentment.** We live out these beliefs in our everyday situations and relationships. And they are *false* beliefs.

But they don't seem false to us. They might be beliefs that we don't even know we have. Over time, these beliefs are reinforced by many influences. Our false beliefs (our wrong thinking) result in self-defeating behaviors and damaging emotions. They are self-focused patterns and strategies.

While our being born again happened **in our spirit**, and our spirit defines who we are, these beliefs were formed in the area **of our soul,** and they are lived out through **our body.**

To illustrate what is being said here, we need to understand a little about the make-up of humans – The way we are.

Humans consist of three parts*: spirit, soul and body* (Hebrews 4:12, 1 Thessalonians 5:23), with the spirit being the empowering force in them and their basic nature or identity. We ARE spirit beings. Our spirit *empowers us and determines who we are. It is our identity.* We also HAVE a soul, or psyche', area which consists of our mind, will and emotions. When scripture speaks of our 'heart', it is usually referring to our soul – our *mind, our beliefs or attitude. The soul area is not transformed at the new birth; only the spirit is changed.* And we LIVE IN a body, the third part of our being. Old beliefs and programming in our soul is lived out though our body.

Even after we have been born again and indwelled and empowered by God's Spirit rather than by sin, the old patterns of thinking and behaving that have been established in the soul / mind area can remain. And as long as we walk after (live by) those old ways that the Scripture refers to as *walking after the flesh*, **we block our experience of Christ's Life that resides in our spirit.** These old ways are the baggage we carry, and it hinders us from enjoying our inheritance from God in daily life.

The Word tells those of us who have become new creations that all of our needs are supplied in Christ. But our fleshly patterns hinder or block us from that being our *experience*. Walking according to fleshly beliefs is all about self. It is to live independently of God, and we experience the consequences of that.

The Greek definition of the word *flesh* that is referred to in this book means almost literally, *"trying to make life work the best way I know how"*. Many of us have believed that to live after the flesh only means immorality, "smokin', lyin', drinkin' and runnin' around". But when we *live after the flesh*, our old learned ways to make life work for us *can* look good and be well-intentioned, even religious–as shown in a previous chart. It can be a way of life full of wonderful goals and accomplishments. But this life can be driven by *pride and fear.* And it never ultimately brings what we need and long for.

Scripture refers to these good or bad works of the flesh as *dead works*. We *can* continue to draw conclusions and develop false beliefs in our soul after we are born of the Spirit. *Works of the flesh do not originate from, or reflect, who we are as new creations.*

Because of our new birth, we have been empowered by God's Spirit to choose to *focus on scriptural Truth. In doing so, we let go of our false mind-set / attitude about who we are and how needs are to be met.* **As a result, our old ineffective patterns of trying to find peace and fulfillment can be changed.** Scripture refers to this change as being transformed by the renewing of our mind. Romans 12:2 This being transformed is the will of God for us.

Our power to face trials and be comforted, our healing, and our transformation does not happen by "behavior modification". It does not happen by trying to live by Biblical old covenant laws. It doesn't happen by religious works.

It is an *internal* process. Our reliance on our old mind-set/ thinking must be broken. And It happens by our learning to live focusing on *the Spirit (on Truth) rather than on my old ways of trying to make life work. **In doing so, hindrances are removed that block Christ's life, power and healing in us from being lived out and experienced by us and through us. And this is God's very will and calling for believers.*** Scripture refers to *this growth process* of renewing our mind as *sanctification*.

This is a BIG concept. And adversity is the setting that prompts this change to happen.

But even knowing all of that, we hold very tightly to the familiar – those old fleshly patterns of thinking and behaving. And we do not turn loose of them easily. **We must be prepared to face our hard times with a different mind-set.**

The charts in the **Appendix** of this book are practical illustrations of the three-part human. **The first chart pictures one who is "born in Adam" – not born again.** This person walks IN the flesh.

The second chart shows a person who IS born again – born of the Spirit – a New Creation with Christ's indwelling Life, but whose flesh patterns block or hinder Christ's life from flowing out where it can be experienced by the person and others. **This individual is walking / living AFTER the flesh** and often holding very tenaciously to old beliefs. He/she has not begun renewing the mind to truth.

The third chart shows a person who is A New Creation and who is walking after the Spirit, bearing the fruit of the Spirit.

7

Be a Prepper

Knowing that trials come to all, we have to get ready for those hard times…… by being *preppers*.

In order that the adversity would break our tight hold on our fleshly strategies so Christ will appear through us and we would know Him and experience the fullness of His blessings, *we must know how to respond to trials*. There are some points we need to know to **prepare our minds** for this. So we need to be *preppers*.

The first and second points have been discussed. They are:

1. Believers need to know their identity in Christ. They are **new creations with Christ's Life and Power indwelling them, and they are forgiven, one with Him and righteous in Him.** They need to also *know* God is their provision and protection.

2. We are to **not be surprised by the fiery ordeal as if some strange thing is happening to us.** Rather we need to be ready and watchful, knowing the testing WILL come.

Our trials and hard times can be fiery at times. At times, maybe we even feel we are in a type of war. And we believe the battle is with other people. But Ephesians 6:12 tells us that "..our struggle is not against flesh and blood, but against the rulers, against the powers, against the world forces of this darkness, against the spiritual *forces* of wickedness in the heavenly *places*."

So we struggle. And it is warfare. But 2 Corinthians 10:4 tells us that *the weapons of our warfare* are not of flesh (meaning not things of the visible world), but are divinely powerful for the destruction of fortresses (in the spiritual realm). God has given us the armor we need to fight these spiritual battles. And since our struggle in the hard times is spiritual, we must be equipped with spiritual armor.

At the beginning of 1 Peter 4, the believers are encouraged **to arm themselves.** It says, "...as Christ hath suffered for us in the flesh, arm yourselves likewise with the same mind." (KJV) The reason they need to be armed is so they will be prepared and protected when the trial comes and so they will live out and experience the will of God. *What kind of armor* was Peter talking about?

The armor is a mind-set or heart attitude. It is INNER armor. It is spiritual armor for spiritual protection. *It is to arm one's self with the same mind-set that Christ had when He lived, suffered and died for us.* We are to put on the mind of Christ–and for the same purpose as He. That purpose is to do and to exhibit the will of God and experience His best for us.

It is a new way of thinking.

This is a HUGE truth.

But what IS the mind-set or attitude of Christ? Philippians 2:5-8 states that we are to *let this attitude be in us that was also in Christ Jesus:*

Christ knew who He was. *And because of that,* He emptied or *humbled Himself* and became of no reputation, meaning He didn't need to be recognized, take credit, or be highly regarded. He *became a bond-servant*, and *humbled Himself to the extent of being obedient to the point of death.*

Think about it. **This is an image of who God is.** And it is the very likeness of Christ, an attitude of sacrifice and putting others first. It is to humble one's self. It is to love and serve others. Letting this mind-set be in us (in our soul area) is to *put on the armor of light.*
Romans 13: 11-12

We must know our identity in Christ, just as He knew who He was. Letting this same mind be in us that is in Christ is also referred to as *putting on the new self which in the likeness of God has been created in holiness.* **We are to put on the new self**, which is being renewed according to the image of the One who created him. Ephesians 4:24, Colossians 3:10-12, Romans 13:14 Putting on this new attitude or mind-set is *to be who we already are* as new creations! It is our *soul* being conformed to the likeness of Christ. And it is our armor, our protection.

And this is *our protection* in adversity? Yes it is.

We are to face persecution, pain and hard times with this attitude. Right now many are thinking, "But I am not God. I can't DO that!"

Well, exactly.

We can't–except by the power of His life in us. That is the reason we first need to know we have been made new creations with Christ residing in our spirit, being one with Him–joined with Him. Because His mind-set–His likeness–lives *in our spirit*, He is our power to choose to be transformed by *putting on* our new self (that same thinking) in the area *of our soul. This is when we renew our mind to truth. It is when we focus on walking after the Spirit, and our walk after the flesh is being left behind.* Galatians 5:16

Without Him, we can do nothing. John 15:5 By His life and power in us, we are able to *take on* that attitude in our soul–our mind–area. But we need some prods or goads to move us to the point of living out of that mind-set. **The trials that come are the very instruments or prods needed to bring us to focus on renewing our mind to these truths as we relinquish reliance on old ways of thinking.** Before and after we know truth, we often kick against those goads. We resist them. The hard times with unfairness and perhaps injustice are our cross so to speak. And often we do not want to go there and walk through them with the attitude of Christ. But when we do, it is our *dying to* the former self-centered beliefs and resulting behaviors we cling to so tightly.

The choice isn't always easy, and we may not *feel* like making that choice during a trial, especially if our strategies seem right to us. Our emotions and pride can prevent us from going there. But we must choose to go anyway. Even Jesus chose to go to the cross when He didn't want to. But He told His Father, "Nevertheless not as I will, but as thou wilt." Matthew 26:39

When we receive the difficulty and respond with the heart of a servant, and with gentleness and humility, we are willing for failures and weaknesses to be exposed as we lose reliance on prideful ways. It is when we relinquish walking after our "own understanding." It is making a choice not to seek acceptance by our performance and not to retaliate nor justify ourselves. It is to love others with God's love. This does not mean we shouldn't clarify our intentions to others if necessary.

It is to swallow the bitter cup, whether it is false accusation, being misunderstood, being rejected, or suffering loss. *What seems like death to us can actually bring forth our experience of life and freedom.* But this is when we are setting our mind on "things above" or on a higher plane than the ways of the world. It is opposite and paradoxical to the world's way of thinking. *We gain by losing.*

Yes, in our learning to think this way, it can *feel* scary. And it may not make sense to our own reason. But we walk through that fear, because it doesn't represent truth. As with Christ, our suffering will seem insignificant compared to His glory, comfort and joy that will be revealed in and through us. Colossians 3:4. His Life will appear outwardly for us, as well as others, to experience.

Remember this is speaking of our *internal* discipline rather than external works. Please understand this is a lifetime journey. It is a process of our learning and growing up to maturity in Christ. We will fall down on our way. And we may skin our knees. But we will get back up and start again as we learn perseverance–the importance of continuing, pressing on and not giving up. As we are perfected (mature) in this love, our fears will be driven out. 1 John 4:18

I should explain this is in no way speaking of a "grit your teeth and bear it" or martyr mind-set nor is it a victim mentality. It does not mean staying in abusive situations. It doesn't mean we are not to defend or explain ourselves, if expedient.

We must receive the adversities of life as instruments for our being broken of those learned and ineffective ways of trying to gain security, significance and peace "the best way we know how". They are opportunities for us to be transformed by the renewing of our minds to truth and be conformed (in our soul) to the image of Christ.
Romans 8:29. Philippians 3:10

So we must resolve to receive the trials.

When I have explained these truths of receiving adversity to those I counsel, a few have expressed concern that if they agreed to receive the trial, it might mean the Lord would then send some catastrophe or unbearable circumstance to them. But, the fact is, the very problem they were facing at the time was the trial the Lord desired to use in their life as an opportunity to apprehend the fullness of freedom and joy that was already theirs in Christ.

To summarize, the third and fourth points in our being prepared for trials are:

3. **We are to arm ourselves with the mind of Christ**–love, humility, forgiveness, sacrifice and the heart of a servant, being willing to *die to* (separate from) or *relinquish* self-protective, self-promoting ways. This is our armor of protection. To do this, we must be in the Word and know the truth. The full armor is described in Ephesians 6:13-17.
4. **Resolve to receive the trial when it comes**, and to replace our old mind-set and thinking with the same attitude as Christ. This is to take every thought captive to the obedience of Christ. 2 Corinthians 10:5

8

Prepped and Ready

Sometimes if we are misunderstood or another person spreads their speculations about us, or if we are plotted against, judged, put down, or treated with injustice from people, especially if we are Christians, we can feel ashamed. But 1 Peter 4:16 says, "If anyone suffers as a Christian, **he is not to be ashamed** or embarrassed, but is to glorify God in this name." So not being ashamed is an important point.

We may think this means *because* one is walking as a Christian with the mind of Christ, he or she will be persecuted. And that might happen. But scripture lets us know that if we wish to live Godly, persecution is the instrument *to bring us to* the point of surrender and putting on that Godliness – our being conformed the image, or the mind, of Christ. "Everyone who wants to live as God desires (wants to live Godly) in Christ Jesus will be persecuted." 2 Timothy 3:12 It is so that His righteousness would be revealed through us. Matthew 5:10 And that we would mature in holiness.

Being conformed to Christ's image–**our being transformed by the renewing of our mind**–is *the will of God for us.* Romans 12:2 And it happens in response to adversity as well as in normal everyday interactions. This is amazing. Even the word, *repentance*, means *turning around **by a change of mind!***

It may not be a wild-fire type of suffering that we go through. Or it might be. Or it could be a small repetitive thing that can lead us to a place of choosing to lay down our own agenda and focus on responding with Christ's attitude. *The battlefield is in the mind.*

James 1:2 gives another point for us to remember. "**Consider it all joy**, my brethren, when you encounter various trials, knowing the testing of your faith produces endurance. And let endurance have its perfect result, so that you may be perfect and complete, lacking in nothing." (Here *perfect* means spiritually mature.)

The Apostle Peter said, "but to the degree that you share the sufferings of Christ, **keep on rejoicing**, so that also at the revelation of His glory you may rejoice with exultation." 1 Peter 4:13 The word, *suffer,* means to undergo inner or outer distress. *One of the rewards* of the right response is that **Christ's glory will be revealed in and through us.** Yes. Right here in our daily walk on earth.

Most of us can't imagine choosing to be joyful in a trial. But we are told in 1 Peter 1:6, "In this you **greatly rejoice, even though now for a little while, if necessary, you have been distressed by various trials."** Notice he said we will have trials for a little while, *if necessary*. But I know well how we can struggle because we want to know "why" it is necessary.

And Paul tells the people in 2 Corinthians that **in a great ordeal of affliction, their abundance of joy and deep poverty resulted in *a wealth of freedom for them.*** They gave of themselves for the good of others. The outcome was they walked in great inner freedom! It was to their benefit. And so it will be for us as we walk in the same way.

Rejoice in the Lord always. I will say it again: Rejoice! Let your gentleness be evident to all. The Lord is near. Do not be anxious about anything, but in everything, by prayer and petition, with thanksgiving, present your requests to God. And the peace of God, which transcends all understanding, will guard your hearts and your minds in Christ Jesus. And my God will meet all your needs according to his glorious riches in Christ Jesus. Phil. 4:4-7,19

How many of us rejoice when hard times come? Seriously. We usually put out the word that we need prayer. And we should pray. But we beg God to fix our situation and we agonize to him over and over. And are anxious...the opposite of being joyful!

So the next two points for us to get into our heart are:

5. **Do not be ashamed** if you are a believer and undergoing pain. There is a reason for it.
6. **Rejoice through the hard time**. It won't last forever. Keep reminding yourself it is for God's purpose to work His will – the mind of Christ–in you. And He will be revealed in you and you will filled with His abundant peace, joy and righteousness.

Keep on *prepping*. Be Equipped.

We can be burned by hard times. Scripture asks us where we will stand when the trial comes. Will it be an instrument to push us toward growth and blessings in Christ or will we be devastated by the test? Of course we are told in the Word to be sure not to suffer as a consequence of doing evil or because we sin.

The last point I will mention is that we need be prepared in our mind **to *continue* – to persevere** – until the end of the test. If we aren't girded up and equipped ahead of time in how to encounter the hard times of life when they come, we could be crushed and brought to despair or depression, or to even anger, by them rather than enduring through them in faith.

We must endure, continuing steadfast in faith for *the purpose of the testing to be accomplished* in us. Colossians 1: 22-23 We must keep on *trekking* through the conflict with the mind of Christ.

Hebrews 3:14 For we are made partakers of Christ, if we hold the beginning of our confidence steadfast unto the end *(of the testing)*; While it is said, Today if ye will hear his voice, *harden not your hearts,* (KJV) We are to learn to remain steadfast through it. Blessed is a man **who perseveres under trial**; for once he has been approved, *he will receive the crown of life*, which *the Lord* has promised to those who love Him. James 1:12. We will begin *to partake of that fullness of life* even as we walk on this earth.

"….let us run **with endurance** the race that is set before us, **fixing our eyes on Jesus,** the author and perfecter of faith, who for the joy set before Him endured the cross, despising the shame, and has sat down at the right hand of the throne of God. Hebrews 12: 1-2 Do not throw away your confidence in the truth, which has a great reward. For you have need of **endurance,** so that *when you have done this will of God, you may partake of the reward.* Hebrews 10:35-36 The testing is to **produce endurance** in us. James1:2

The *reward* is enjoying God's promises that are already yours in Christ. We **must persevere with that mind of Christ**, which is choosing humility, kindness, the heart of a servant, putting others before one's self–all paradoxical to the world's way of thinking. It was already mentioned that this is God's will for us. And by this we can silence the ignorance of foolish people. 1 Peter 2:15 That is certainly not the way the world system does things.

And the seventh main point we need to be prepared is:

7. We must persevere through the trial.

It is by our choosing this attitude of Christ, that we prevent ourselves from being conformed to this world, but are transformed by the renewing of our mind, **so that we may prove what the will of God is**, that which is good, acceptable and perfect. Romans 12:2 In order **to endure** and move forth in this, we have to remember that God is our provider, our protection and our strength.

Therefore, after all has been said, 1 Peter 1:13 can sum it up as we are told to **prepare our minds for action**. "Prepare your minds for action, keep sober in spirit, fix your hope completely on the grace to be brought to you at the revelation of Jesus Christ." This word *revelation* means when He is revealed in us for others to see. The KJV says to *"gird up the loins" of our minds*.

We can't procrastinate and wait to gird up our thinking until we are blind-sided by either a large or small test. We need to be preparing ahead of time by meditating on these things in advance. Because a small test comes in an instant, for example, when a significant other opposes us, or is resistant to something we feel is urgent, or does something embarrassing, etc. How would we respond? Not well, if we aren't ready.

Since being conformed to the same mind-set as Christ is so imperative for believers, we will look at this attitude more in depth in the next chapter.

9

The Attitude of Christ

In order to abide in–continue in and practice (live out)– being armed with the mind (attitude) of Christ, one must understand this walk doesn't take place by just mental re-programming or by behavior modification. By the power of Christ's Spirit and Life in us, it is a inner discipline to press on in *focusing* on truth, on *things above, as we face trials and live in daily life and relationships.*

This discipline is choosing to rely on Christ's person, power and promises as we allow His attitude or His likeness to be lived out. This is **obedience** and **"putting on" our new self.** Ephesians 4:24; Colossians 3:10 When we are born of the Spirit, our new self, or new nature, is created in the *likeness* of God in righteousness and holiness of the truth. Ephesians 4: 23-24 The exhortation to put on the new self means to be transformed in our mind (our soul / heart) to that *likeness* of God who dwells in our Spirit. Romans 12:2, 2 Corinthians 3:18 It is a process. And it is when Christ is formed in us, Galatians 4:19 and His likeness is revealed through us as we face trials and our normal daily circumstances. Colossians 3:4 When we are putting on the new self, we are walking after the Spirit.

The Likeness of God

Jesus told His disciples that when they *saw Him*, they were *seeing the Father* and if they came to *know Him*, they would *know the Father* God! John14:7 He said He and the Father God *are one*. John 10:30 Jesus is the radiance of His Father's glory and the exact representation of His nature. Hebrews1:3a They saw, and we can see, the **likeness of God** the Father when we see Christ in scripture.

How do we describe the likeness – the heart / mind / power of God? It is revealed in the mind-set of Christ. And we are told to let this same mind be in us also. Philippians 2:5-8 This attitude of Christ *is just the opposite* of the natural way or world's way of thinking. It is seen in His choosing to empty Himself (become of no reputation, KJV), take the form of a bond-servant, and humble Himself by becoming obedient to the point of death. **This is** *the likeness of God.* And it is **Godliness.**

The Attitude / Mind of Christ = God's Likeness:

* **He emptied Himself.** Being fully God *and* fully man, Christ *had no sin or fleshly ways* to void Himself of. But He emptied Himself as He lay aside His importance. Christ chose to become as one without distinction or honor among people. He was willing to be disregarded. He didn't try to protect or promote His reputation or justify Himself. He did not protest because he was mistreated. He didn't try to "save face" or His physical life even though he could. He did not do this on His own initiative, but by the power of the Father working in Him. John 5:30; 8:28; 8:42

* **He took the attitude of a bond-servant.** In Roman times, the term *bond-servant* could refer to someone who voluntarily

served others. A bond-servant is a person devoted to another to the disregard of one's own interests and who voluntarily **submits to and serves** others, regarding others as more important than him/herself. Mark 10:45; Luke 22:27 The word *bond-servant* comes from the Greek word *doulos*, Being a bond-servant does not mean being a "people-pleaser" who tries to find acceptance, peace and worth by "pleasing" others. Ephesians 6:6 Good-looking outer behaviors may OR may not come from a heart that is being transformed to the mind-set of Christ.

* **He humbled Himself.** He didn't try to elevate Himself or find approval and significance by His performance or from people. When he was insulted, He didn't try to "win", or demand His rights to be respected as God. He didn't take up offenses, retaliate or return insults for insults. He blessed those who cursed Him. Christ didn't brag. He chose to be meek, gentle and patient. Matthew 11:29

Think about it. This attitude of Christ is the likeness of God–a picture of God Himself–a description of the Power of God–the *power* that created all that was created and works all things after the counsel of His will! This mind-set describes the *power* of light itself. John 1: 9-10 Those words in Philippians 2: 5-8 describe His *power* on the cross over all the powers of the enemy. Jesus demonstrated that His power of overcoming is found in "losing"– in humility and submission–that seeming paradox.

The mind of Christ – His attitude – is really the essence of ***LOVE, which is the likeness of God and the power in all of God's attributes.*** God's nature is described in various ways. Good. Faithful. Just. A Shield. Sovereign. Holy. Righteous. Unchanging. All knowing. All Powerful. Present everywhere. Scripture says that all things were made subject to Him. And **God is Love.** 1

John 4:8 **Walking in His likeness is to Love**. Love perseveres, is patient, kind, isn't prideful, isn't easily provoked, and forgives. 1 Corinthians 13 And loving is our inner obedience of faith. The word obedience means, "to listen under" God and truth.

10

The Baggage

On our journey in ordinary daily life we often don't recognize where the real problem lies. We see our problems–our baggage–as other people or various hindrances to our having things the way we think they should be. People sometimes look for something deep and traumatic as the root of their problem, when they are standing right in the middle of one or more of *their own issues* that are wrecking havoc in their lives.

Frequently believers feel justified in their frustrations, resentments and anger. It doesn't occur to them this mentality stems from wrong thinking about how needs are to be met and it reinforces innate pride and actually creates all manner of trouble. Resentments and anger hurt the person who is resentful.

I personally have had to learn to trust the Lord that I will be fine regardless of the situation. But it usually takes time and my persevering through a hard circumstance while trusting before I *feel* His peace. One of my "fleshly" beliefs has been, "My actions and words must not be misunderstood." This belief was only one that made the weight in my baggage.

The Purpose of Trials and Adversity

Why did I have that belief? I have learned that my fear of rejection and of life going wrong is ultimately behind it. I think the belief fits under the need for *security*. And for many years I lived out of beliefs that were associated with that such as, "I must try hard to clarify myself, be emotionally guarded and not be open in relationships or express myself to stay safe." So what has the Lord allowed in my life? Being misunderstood. But WHY?

It isn't just a matter of trusting I will be okay and that God will give me all I need. That is just the beginning. The fact is, He *has already given* all things that pertain to life and Godliness to those who are born of His Spirit. We just *may not be partaking* of those good things.

So God has *allowed the natural occurrence of being misunderstood* as His instrument–His goad to frustrate me–to *break my reliance on my own false belief that I must avoid being misunderstood to be secure. I am to lay aside this baggage* as I rely on the truth that HE is my security. My own ways–my baggage–blocked my full experience of my needs being met in Him, and at the same time it was the root of my fears!

The Christian life is to first *trust* that the Lord is my power, protection, provision and sufficiency. Most believers stop there. *But then it is to go further as I trust*. Going further is choosing to respond with the attitude of Christ to those who have misunderstood me or put me down. This is an inner discipline to humble myself, have the attitude of a servant, and put those others before myself. **This is the door to *experience* the fullness of freedom, provision and sufficiency that is already mine in Christ.** It is choosing, growing, and pressing-on as I learn to live with His mind-set. Then I enter into and enjoy God's best. And it is far above all I can ask or think. This is God's desire for me.

The Baggage

So our trials and adversities are in areas reciprocal to (that correspond to) our false beliefs and the ways we've developed **to make ourselves and others secure, find significance and be content**. What do you try to do, or rely on, to stay secure, be content and find significance? **Your trials have been, and will be, perfectly suited to break your old patterns of self-reliance in those particular areas.** We bring our own ways and responses into every trial.

While being misunderstood might create severe problems in one's life, community and circumstances, it is a trial of glowing embers compared to other difficulties people face that are like raging wild-fires.

It is puzzling why God would allow terminal illness, abuse, the suicide of a loved one, the loss of a job, or the loss of every material possession one has by a natural disaster. And we wonder why there are those who must take care of disabled or resistant family members where the focus mentally and physically has to be constantly on meeting the needs of those individuals. It is draining in all ways and affects many. Then there are those who may experience persecution with physical and mental torture and deprivation. But why?

I haven't been through physical torture and cannot comprehend how horrible it is. But I know for Christian believers, all trials whether they be fiery or not, are to be *for Christ's sake*. This means that through it all we are to trust in His sufficiency for us and respond with His attitude. When we do this, His life and power will be experienced by us and manifest in and through us so others might see God. This is the will of God. I know this is what the Word teaches us. Unless we are prepped and ready and focused on allowing Christ's life to be lived out, we can be devastated when the adversity comes.

In the process of our focusing on trusting God and responding correctly to hard times, our heavy baggage is left behind.

11

Leave The Baggage

How many of us know that *being prepared* and *putting on Christ's attitude* IS to live the Christian life? Our everyday journey in the Christian life is to continually receive God's grace and choose this inner mind-set–not just in the hardest times.

God's will is that the same attitude of humility and kindness, the heart of forgiveness, the attitude of a servant, and denial of our inner self-life be ongoing. In the New Testament, believers were called "Christians" when they were in this walk after the spirit.

When the actions of others aren't right or fair, this may sound like too much for us–unless we know it is *only by Christ's Life and Power in us* that we can choose to walk this way. Otherwise we might have a tendency to *harden our hearts* and continue trying to meet inner needs, protect ourselves and fight battles by our own fleshly patterns–*the way of the world*–which is heavy baggage.

Some examples of *ways of the world system* are that people return insult for insult and demand respect by force. The world's way is to try to control others, have to win arguments, gossip, withdraw, or sit in a chair refusing to be inconvenienced by making an inner choice to voluntarily get up and serve another. It may be our trying to fix and rescue others, working harder on their problems than they do. It can be trying to make sure that everyone and everything is functioning perfectly in order for self to look good and have a feeling of control or feel secure. It could include having to be right, being critical, judgmental, having the last word, or being demanding and rigid. Or it might be having lots of "rules" for yourself and others and believing those who fail deserve to be punished. It may mean pleasing others to avoid conflict, find acceptance and fit in.

This *wisdom of the world* can also include using guilt and shame to manipulate others to get what you want. Or even using humor to cover up pain or hurt feelings. Being passive and withdrawing from others to avoid getting hurt is a way of the world. Dependence on others' opinions and living as an extension of their opinions of you is another fleshly pattern. It is even trying to force legislation of attitudes in order to get respect. The world's way also makes demands to be treated fairly.

These are never-ending battles that we never win. **They are all about self, and they backfire on us.** And it is heavy baggage. It is a weight we carry that easily hinders us from experiencing the freedom and fullness that is already ours in Christ. Hebrews 12:1 KJV

These and other various fleshly patterns result from our own false beliefs about how to meet needs of worth, fill longings and be safe. Our false beliefs are behind all of this striving and these strategies. It is to live by worldly wisdom, which might make sense to us and even look good. This **walking after the flesh** is to be wise in our own eyes and to walk after our own understanding. Isaiah 5:21. Proverbs 12:15 But it is opposite than living from God's truth

We are to be wise *(with God's wisdom)* and *cease from striving* to live life according to the wisdom of this world, which often looks nice and moral. 1 Corinthians 1:20 KJV asks, "Where is the wise? Where is the scribe? Where is the disputer of this world? Hath not God made foolish the wisdom of this world?

We are to lay aside every weight. Hebrews 12:1 "Therefore, since we have so great a cloud of witnesses surrounding us, let us also **lay aside** every encumbrance and the sin which so easily entangles us, and let us **run with endurance** the race that is set before us." But just how do we "cease from striving"? How do we "lay aside the weight"–the baggage? How do we "let go" of the fleshly mind-set? How do we "surrender our self-life" to walk in the likeness of Christ?

Hard times are for *the purpose of bringing us to a place of our hold on fleshly ways being broken and to our trusting God.* But our FOCUS *can not be on trying to put away our walk after the flesh*–those old beliefs and behaviors we have relied on for so long.

I have sometimes explained that it is similar to learning a new language. Let's say you move to another country where no one speaks your language, and you must learn the new language to survive. The mind isn't going to be set on laying aside the old. It will, of necessity, be **focused on learning the new**. And it is a process. Sometimes you will return to the old, but it isn't helpful. So you re-focus and continue to learn and practice the new. In doing so, you "let go" of reliance on the old way. It will be set aside. This is when we *die to* or separate from the old.

One's mind has to be set on renewing itself to truth. And in the process, our old thinking is taken captive *by* our *putting on the new* – the truths of God's provision, our new identity on Him, and the same attitude as Christ. 2 Corinthians 10:5 This is when we are being transformed and conformed to His image. This is to walk

after the spirit. *Walk by (focus on) the spirit and you won't fulfill the desires of the flesh.*
Galatians 5:16

It may seem strange, but as has been said, the way of the Kingdom of God and its Truth is PARADOXICAL (an enigma or absurdity) to the world system. We find by losing. We surrender to experience freedom. We become weak to be strong. We humble ourselves to be exalted.

A Paradox

We must:

Die *to* **Live**
Lose *to* **Find**
Decrease *to* **Increase**
Surrender *to* **be Free**
Be Broken *to* **be Whole**
Be Empty *to* **be Full**
Be Weak *to* **be Strong**
Give *to* **Receive**
Rest *to* **Have Victory**
Work *to* **Rest**
Rest *to* **Work**
Be Humbled *to* **be Exalted**
Sacrifice *to* **be Fulfilled**

Living paradoxically to the world system is not passivity. **It refers to the internal.** It involves inner choices to focus on Truth, receive our cross (trial) and relinquish reliance on our ways of trying to make life work, even if they look good and make sense, to depend on God's indwelling life and power.

In order to do this, we must set our mind on, and take every thought captive to, Christ's obedience – His mind-set of love, humility and service. In the process, our heavy bags filled with pride will be left behind.

Adapted from Kay Ruff. By permission.

12

But How Is It Done?

Just how do we set our mind on these *things above*–on a higher plane–while we have to live in this world and think about doing chores, going to work, paying the bills.... and golfing?

We do not have to be continually repeating scripture to ourselves every minute of the day as some may think. But meditating daily on Truths ("things above") that have been mentioned helps us be prepared. As stated in previous chapters, we must trust in God's provision and protection for us. We must know Christ is our new life and power source and dwells in us. And as we continue to recall what the mind (the likeness or image) of Christ is, and are preparing ourselves to respond with that attitude, *it will innately come to our awareness* when we face ordinary times, a stressful situation as maybe an argument, or when we are facing other difficulties, or if we need it–on the golf course.

We will be reminded by the Spirit in us to humbly refrain from our old ways of interacting. Of course we must be sensitive to *hearing* the Spirit. It may *feel* threatening and a little fearful to go to this unfamiliar place, but when we walk through it, we grow, and the reward will be well worth the choice. This doesn't mean that we won't fall down and have an old automatic response, but we will be reminded again of truth and we will get back up and walk the path.

It is costly to go on this path of focusing on truth. We have to lose something. We become living sacrifices. Romans 12:1 We choose to lose, or let go of, our controls and self-preserving strategies, humbling ourselves and sacrificing our self-life. This means to be brought low and decrease in importance instead of trying to be noticed or prove I am right. This is the mind-set of Christ. When we first begin this journey, it may feel like we are disappearing or have no value to anyone. As one of our grandsons said, "This is serious heart surgery."

But to die *to* my ways is gain. Philippians 1:21 This leads to REAL power–God's power expressed in my life. And it is a fight of faith–of choosing to believe God. But the battle is the Lord's, and He wins. And we win. And the *feelings* of joy, peace, and being right with God will eventually follow. Instead of fighting by the world's rules, 1 Timothy 6:12 tells us to "Fight the good fight of faith; **take hold of the eternal life** to which you were called…"

We must practice this inner obedience of faith (discipline) if we are to let-go of our internal struggle to "fix" life, which includes trying to control circumstances, and others' words and actions so things will go well. It is to relinquish blame, defensiveness, retaliation, and our rights, as we *put on the new self…* that attitude of Christ. **God allows us to go through hard times to learn to exercise** this *obedience of faith.* It is the very obedience to which we are called.

So be encouraged to persevere in faith through trials and conflict, which are considered *times of training in righteousness.* Just remember when we press on with our heart fixed on Truth, that weeping may endure for a night, but joy comes in the morning. Psalm 30:5

Going through a test may *feel* threatening, but since I know I am joined with Christ and we both are hidden in God, I am safe. I

But How Is It Done?

can even walk through the fire and not be burned. I am protected. He is my strength and deliverer. Psalm 18:2 He is my provider. We can be very tempted to respond out of our emotions–our feelings. But we must remember feelings don't determine who we are and can't be trusted.

Recently I was talking with a believer who has been in church all of his life and has read the Bible or Christian literature almost every day for years. He had always tried to do what is right and led a moral life. He is retired and was telling how he was just now realizing he had walked by feelings all of his life. And without considering what he was doing, he had made decisions and responded out of the way **he felt**. He was letting his perception of others' responses and attitudes control him.

His inclination was to interpret others actions as rejection, so he had learned to withdraw and put up walls to avoid getting hurt. He had believed feelings represented the truth. But now, he is learning truth and has begun doing what *feels* risky. He is letting down walls and responding with the attitude of Christ. He says he already has more joy and peace than in all of the previous years of his life.

Choosing to walk with the mind of Christ is the very expression of **love** as we live in life and relationship to one another. God IS love. And the mind of Jesus is the exact representation of who the Father God is. They are one. When we love others, we live out the mind or likeness of Christ. This renewing of our mind is God's will for us as we live in this world, and it is His plan for our Life.

2 Timothy 1:7 tells us that the (new) Spirit God has given believers is not one of timidity (fear) but of the power, love and discipline that are necessary to live out this life, of which has been written here.

The Purpose of Trials and Adversity

This kind of Love is a mind-set. A choice. It is not a feeling. Whoever loves is born of God and knows Him. 1 John 4:7 God's *agapao'* Love is humble. Love is kind. Love protects. Love doesn't try to force its own way. Love expresses kindness and patience and doesn't repay evil with evil. **We live out Christ's likeness by Love.** And love doesn't need to have a response that is thankful, or builds me up or loves in return. Loving and living with the attitude of Christ is costly–to our flesh. It is being conformed to Christ's death. Philippians 3:10 It is our obedience of faith; our obedience to God.

By refusing to go to this low, perhaps humiliating place, we give place to sins and lusts of the flesh such as being critical, controlling, angry, fighting to be on top, and so on. Allowing ourselves to be humbled by a trial, means we are willing for failure and weakness to be exposed as we lose reliance on pride, and allow ourselves to be emptied of self-effort and being strong in order to achieve something to fill our neediness. *This is breaking down the walls to our receiving good things from Christ's Spirit in us.*

We usually think walking after the flesh and after our lusts just means immorality. But it means walking after any old false programming instead of choosing to walk after the Spirit. To stay in my comfort zone and not be inconvenienced to serve or put another first is a way of walking after lust for comfort. It is lust just as greed, physical lust, or lust for material things.

Walking after the flesh is walking after the way of the world system. 1 John 2:16 tells us "... all that is in the world, the lust of the flesh and the lust of the eyes and the boastful pride of life, is not from the Father, but is from the world."

Whoever exalts himself shall be humbled (abased) and whoever humbles himself will be exalted. Matthew 23:12, Luke 14:11, 18:14 This means we must lose our (fleshly) life to find (His) Life.

Matthew 16:25 "For whoever wishes to save his life will lose it; but whoever loses his life for My sake will find it."

This "low road" of humility is indeed the "high way" of holiness.

Be wise and know there is a *false humility* too.

It may look similar to the real thing if someone backs away from conflict, or is quiet and refrains from bragging, bites their tongue and doesn't argue, or gives to the poor. But if it is false humility, the person has no peace or joy. It is *by their fruit* that you will know if it is real. Real humility is the attitude of Christ and the fruit of the Spirit, which is love–patience, kindness, gentleness, faithfulness, joyfulness and peacefulness.

We can harden ourselves and fight against being broken of our old strategies by the hard times.

We can resist in various ways. A few examples of our being determined to avoid any way we can the humiliation and pain of being broken are: (1) Turning away and hiding from facing or working through conflict and disappointment in relationships. (2) Being dominating–forcing opinions and demands on another. (3) Having to win. (4) Putting up walls and not taking the risks to be known by others. (5) Lying. (6) Trying harder and doing more of the same, only to get more of the same. We may find false relief in coping in these ways, but the result is more bondage.

We can't afford to draw back and refuse to take what on the surface might seem to be the easier road. Luke 9:25 asks a question related to this very thing, "For what is a man profited if he **gains the whole world**, and loses or forfeits himself?" It is to our benefit to make that choice to **lose our fleshly life to gain the experience of His life here and now.** In doing so, we store up for ourselves the treasure of a good foundation for the days to come, so that we may **take hold of that which is life** (Christ's eternal Life) indeed. Timothy 6:19 We long for this quality of life rather than the alternative of living frustrated, fearful and without peace.

There is comfort in knowing it has been granted to us **for Christ's sake** not only to believe in Him, but also to **suffer for His sake**. Philippians 1:29 Suffering "for His sake" means if we suffer unjustly and bear it patiently, this is favorable to God. 1 Peter 2:20 We can be encouraged to know that the person who has been made righteous in Him **will have many hardships, but the Lord delivers Him out of them all.** Psalm 34:19 When we go through any hard times **for His sake**, it also means that not only we, but others, will experience Christ in and through us.

Our believing the truths and choosing the things mentioned here is our **obedience of faith, that inner discipline** to which we are called. It is when we seek and set our minds on things above. Romans 16:26, Colossians 3:1-2 It is by the gift of Christ's faith in us that we can make these inner choices.

The Mind-set of Humility

Losing reliance on one's fleshly life while choosing to live with the Mind of Christ.

1. Presumed "rights", "privileges", and "entitlements surrendered
2. Willing to be rejected
3. Willing to share weaknesses, be transparent
4. Willing to not have to prove you're right
5. Recognizing total inadequacy in old strategies
6. Trusting in Christ's adequacy, His strength
7. Obeying out of a love motive because I want to, not because I have to
8. Trusting that God is your refuge, even in external turmoil
9. Willing for the Lord to fulfill you rather than seeking fulfillment in a person or your performance
10. Willing to serve and build up others, esteeming them better than yourself
11. Willing to fail or appear a failure
12. Willing to let others receive credit
13. Willing to be humbled, to receive others with their imperfections
14. Willing to receive your trial as God's instrument to mature you
15. Willing to not be defensive or to justify yourself
16. Willing not to speculate or "mind-read" motives
17. Relinquishing control, fixing and directing
18. Willing to be misunderstood
19. Willing to not be defensive
20. Willing to become "of no reputation" –KJV

As a born again believer begins to focus on the truth of Christ's life in him/ her and his/her freedom from the power of sin, then chooses to allow the "testings" of life to work in him/her so that *reliance* on fleshly (false) beliefs and the resulting behaviors is **broken,** then **surrenders** those dependencies with a mind-set of *humility*, we see an individual who is **walking after the Spirit**–meaning living in the Truth. The believer is "ceasing from his own works". The "childish things" are being put away, etc. **When this happens, Christ's life flows out and "appears" through us to others.** It is when we bear the fruit of the Spirit. The importance of this is that it is our very calling as believers. It is God's will and purpose for us so we will experience His best in our lives.

13

God's Awesome Purposes

When we persevere through trials as well as ordinary days learning to respond with the mind of Christ, we put on our new self that was created in the likeness of God. This results in reliance on our flesh being laid aside. Ephesians 4:24, Colossians 3:10 This is God's purpose for us now as we live on earth. His intention and will for us also includes incredible blessings.

Christians have often believed the rewards they will receive, and all of the glory to be revealed, will be in the hereafter. But *God's awesome purpose is that we would begin to enjoy the rewards of our inheritance now while we live **in our mortal bodies.***

The apostle Paul speaks of believers being afflicted in every way, but not crushed; perplexed, but not despairing; persecuted, but not forsaken; struck down, but not destroyed; always carrying about in the body the dying of Jesus, *so that* the life of Jesus also may be manifested in our body. For we who live are constantly being delivered over to death for Jesus' sake, **so that the life of Jesus would be** *manifest* **in our** *mortal* **flesh** (body). 2 Corinthians 4: 8-11

This is speaking of Godliness, and it is profitable for all things, since it holds **promise for** *the present life* and also for the life to come. 1 Timothy 4:8 Fighting that fight of faith through difficult times as we humble ourselves, die to old ways, and put on the mind / likeness of Christ is the way *we take hold of eternal life* to which we are called. 1 Timothy 6:12 *This living out His likeness is the way we know Him*, and **knowing God is Eternal Life**. John 17:3 *Eternal life is a quality of life* we can experience here and now. He IS eternal life. This is making our calling and election manifest and evident. 2 Peter 1:10-11

This is the way we *experience* all needs being met. It is the way to know comfort, peace and joy and a sense of well-being. And yes, it happens as a result of our response to adversity. He who loves his *(own fleshly)* **life** loses it, and he who hates his **life** in this world will keep it to **life eternal**. John 12: 25 God's desire is that we would lay hold on and experience His gift of salvation and eternal life *as we walk now on the earth*, even though we won't know the completeness of it until we leave our earthly bodies.

As we walk through trials as well as ordinary times, continuing in faith as described in the previous chapters, we obtain as the outcome of our faith, *the salvation of our soul*. 1 Peter 1:9 This means the outworking of our salvation from our spirit into our soul. It is the salvation or deliverance of our mind, will and emotions from darkness, unrest and fear to His peace, joy and righteousness. It is **being transformed by the renewing of our mind** It is also called *sanctification*. It is our soul being **conformed to His image,** and the intention of God for us.

The words, *saved* and *salvation,* spoken of here and as used in the New Testament, encompass both the physical and spiritual dimensions of a person's well-being and healing, being applicable for the whole person. *Salvation* has a wide range of meanings, which include deliverance from enemies, escape, healing of mind and body. It means to be rescued. **It means to *access the grace in which we already stand.*** Romans 5:2 God has *already blessed us* with all things that pertain to life and Godliness and with *all* spiritual blessings. 2 Peter 1:3, Ephesians 1:3

The word, *salvation,* doesn't only mean being regenerated or born –again. That *is* salvation, but it is only one of the various aspects of how the word is used in scripture. Yet regrettably, today the words *salvation* and *saved* are usually used only in the sense of being born-again, rescued from hell and entering the hereafter heaven.

One main meaning of *salvation* is our deliverance from fleshly ways so we might enter (experience) the **Kingdom of God, which is in our midst, inside us.** Luke 17:21 The Kingdom of God is righteousness, joy and peace in the Holy Spirit. Romans 14:17 We are encouraged to *grow in respect to salvation*, and to grow in grace and in this knowing God. 1 Peter 2:2, 2 Peter 3:8

In Acts 14:22, Paul speaks of "strengthening the souls of the disciples, encouraging them to continue in the faith, and *he says*, **"Through many tribulations** we must **enter the kingdom of God."** The terms *kingdom of God* and *kingdom of heaven* are used interchangeably. The terms do not refer only to the hereafter–a place we go to after our bodies die.

It is very important that we consider these broader meanings in order to encourage each other in our spiritual walk, and so we might taste the undeserved reward of our inheritance in the kingdom of heaven now *in this present life.* The word, *reward,* here doesn't mean something we earn. It means that by believing truth and *dying to* (leaving) our self-life, the hindrances to our experiencing or possessing the blessings of Christ's indwelling life and our God-given inheritance, are broken.

When we experience trials, Peter sums it up as he says to be harmonious, sympathetic, brotherly, kindhearted, and humble in spirit; not returning evil for evil or insult for insult, but giving a blessing instead; for you were called *for the very purpose that you might inherit a blessing.* 1 Peter 3:8

Hebrews 6:12 tells believers to be diligent and not be sluggish, but followers of those who through faith and patience *inherit the promises.* Whatever you do, do your work heartily, as for the Lord rather than for men, knowing that from the Lord you will *receive the reward of the inheritance.* Colossians 3: 3,24

We are encouraged in Matthew 6:33 to **seek first His kingdom** and His righteousness, and *all the things we need, we will have*. James tells Christians to consider it all joy when you encounter various trials, knowing that the testing of your faith produces endurance. And let endurance have *its* perfect result, *so that you may be perfect and complete, lacking in nothing.* James 1:2-4

Those who remain steadfast, after they have suffered a while, He will *mature, establish, strengthen and settle.* 1 Peter 5:9-10 Trials and adversities are painful, and they produce sorrow for the moment, but they are for the purpose of teaching us the way of holiness–**so we would share His holiness.** They yield the peaceable fruit of righteousness. Hebrews 12:11

All of this speaks of our experiencing God's awesome purposes for us as we walk on this earth. It is to enjoy His kingdom. To delight in the kingdom of heaven is like a merchant seeking fine pearls, and upon finding one pearl of great value, he went and sold all that he had and bought it. This is a metaphor of our choosing to lose our own fleshly ways to find (experience) Christ's life right here and now. For whoever wishes to save his life will lose it; but whoever loses his life for My sake will find it. Matthew 13:45-46; Matthew 16:25

Paul said, "I am well content with weaknesses, with insults, with distresses, with persecutions, with difficulties, for Christ's sake; for when I am weak, then I am strong." 2 Corinthians 12:10 Many are the afflictions of those who have been made righteous in Christ; but the Lord delivers him out of them all. Psalm 34:19

14

Enter In and Partake

When we receive the hard times of life as training in Godliness and the way to knowing God, we can anticipate many wonderful benefits. The last chapter communicated truths of our entering in and partaking of these blessings. Now we are about to see there are even more awesome outcomes.

Continuing to respond to the large and small crises of life by our old ineffective ways is to go the way of the world system. Remember, the fleshly way may look okay–or even religious, but it eventually leads to gloom, fear, self-condemnation, striving, little peace, and living outside of the freedom we have been given in Christ and our experience of God's best for us.

When we persevere through the inevitable trials with Christ's attitude, it is when we no longer think and act as spiritual children. Ephesians 4:13-15. It is when we grow up and mature in Him. It is when we begin to **partake** of, experience, and display His fullness. And we *enjoy the freedom* that we have been given in Him. It is for this freedom that Christ set us free. Galatians 5:1, Hebrews 3:14 It is when we walk according to the law of the spirit of life in Christ–the perfect law of liberty. James 1:25, Romans 8:2 The law of love. We are called to walk in our freedom as we through love serve one another. Galatians 5:13

It is good to know that Jesus Himself *is glory* and He dwells in us.

Colossians 3 tells us the purpose of being steadfast in allowing the likeness of Christ to be lived out through us is when Christ *who is our life shall be revealed, we shall also be revealed with Him in His glory.* **This means others will see Christ in and through us** and glorify God. And we will be **known as His disciples.** *This is when we let our light shine, which we are to do.* John 13:35, Matthew 5:16 It is when others experience God's goodness through us, *which can lead to their repentance.* Romans 2:4

Sometimes our hard times are a raging fire in our lives. Sometimes they are small pebbles that can trip us on our path. The devil is as a roaring lion seeking whom he may devour by trials large and small. The world's and our own ways of reasoning, and Satan's deceptions, *can* seem so right and make sense to us.

When we receive the oppositions, offenses and trials (take up our cross) **arming ourselves with Christ's mind-set**, we walk in the reality of God's power, with it being revealed / expressed through us. As the veil was torn in the temple and the glory of God shined out when Christ was crucified, so also our veil of flesh will be torn away as we deny ourselves, take up our cross, and follow him in His likeness and attitude. His glory will then shine out through us.

I used to think of ***God's glory*** being a glowing physical light. But *God's glory* is the abundance, strength, beauty–the substance– of Himself; of light, love, grace, sacrifice, protection, provision, peace, kindness, gentleness, humility; everything that describes His likeness, His image. And we are being transformed to that image–from His indwelling glory–to His glory revealed in us. 2

Corinthians 3:18 Believers desire true contentment, peace, and spiritual rest. How many do you know who are experiencing it? Well we **enter in and partake of** this rest for our soul and mind when we put on that mind of Christ in our relationships while persevering and trusting Him for the outcome. Hebrews 4:9-10 says there remains a rest for the people of God. For he **who has *entered into his rest*** has himself also ceased from his *own* (fleshly) works as God did from His. 2 Peter 3:14 Therefore, beloved, since you look for these things, **be diligent** to be **found** by Him *in peace, spotless and blameless.*

Many think to live blamelessly and **pursue Godliness** is behavior modification, or to it is focus on living by religious principles and rules…or that it is being a moral person. But here we have seen it is to put on a heart of serving and loving one another. It is by putting on "a heart (mind) of compassion, kindness, humility, gentleness, and patience; bearing with one another, and forgiving one another just as the Lord has forgiven you." Colossians 12:13 This is God's intention for us. And it is to *be* **holy**. 1 Peter 1:15-16

We are to **discipline ourselves** in this way for the purpose of **Godliness**. 1 Timothy 4:7b It is that inner practice of choosing to focus on truth and *be transformed by the renewing of our mind* to humility, service and love. 2 Peter 3:11 When we walk in humility, we will experience peace and be 'lifted up'. And we will know prosperity. Psalm 37:11, Isaiah 26:3, James 4:10

And persevering in this discipline is not hard, because it is by His Life and Power in us that we choose it. Christ encourages us to take this, His yoke (constraint), which he says **is easy** and His burden (task), which **is light.** He is speaking of our inner choosing to learn from him and put on His mind-set. In Matthew 11: 29-30, He said, "Take My yoke upon you and learn from Me, for I am gentle and humble in heart, and you will find *rest for your souls*. For My yoke is easy and My burden is light."

For they verily for a few days chastened us (by a trial) after their own pleasure; but He for (God used it for) our profit, that we might be **partakers of His holiness.** Hebrews 12:10-11 We are allowed difficult times to bring us to a place of taking His yoke and burden. And in so doing, we serve God and put on His holiness. **This is** *the way of the cross.*

But now being made free from our bondage to sin, and having become servants to God, ye have your fruit **unto holiness**, and the end everlasting life. We will taste of the reward of Godly joy and eternal life now if we don't faint and get tired of this well-doing and give up. Yes, right here on earth, we will *take hold on* a quality of life that is Godly and eternal. Romans 6:22, Galatians 6:7-9

When we walk in this will of God, we will *enter into* the holiest place to experience God's life–*the kingdom of heaven*–in our daily walk. Matthew 19:17,23,24 Remember we are blessed if we have been persecuted for the **sake of** righteousness, for ours is the **kingdom of heaven.** Matthew 5:10 To top it off, we will enjoy a table of good things that God will prepare before us *in the presence* of our enemies. Psalm. 23:5

Looking at the whole picture in perspective can bring us assurance and encouragement when adversity comes. There can be comfort in knowing "to you it has been granted for Christ's sake not only to believe on Him, but also to suffer for His sake." Philippians 1:24

David said, "Many are the afflictions of the righteous, but the Lord delivers him out of them all." Psalm 34:19 And we must know that to suffer unjustly and bear it patiently is what is favorable to God. 1 Peter 2:19,20. In our hard times, it is worth persevering in the truths mentioned in this book. Because if we harden our hearts against receiving adversity with the mind of Christ, we will miss out on *experiencing in our daily lives* the full effectiveness of the promises and the cross. Mark 7:13, 1 Corinthians 1:17 (KJV).

So we must conclude that the highway of holiness is not always the road of comfort, ease, and human optimism expressed in the Irish Blessing. Rather, it is the way of the cross. AND it is the way into the promises, peace, righteousness, joy, and resurrection power experienced as a result of our facing trials, disappointments, loss and rejection with our minds girded with the armor of truth.

15

Is There A Line?

Doing good to those who are unfair to us, and not returning insult for insult, but giving them a blessing instead is so opposite of fleshly thinking or the way of the world system. But does all of this mean we aren't to protect and defend ourselves, and our families, if we are abused, attacked or violated in some way? Does it mean we shouldn't shield ourselves from being scammed or hacked? Is there a line we should draw?

In loving those who do not love us or who have wronged us, we likely will have to lose our pride. When we do, we may *feel* humiliated, embarrassed, maybe overlooked. But if we are ridiculed, rejected or unjust demands are made on us, perhaps even by family members, shouldn't there be some kind of boundary? Is it possible to serve others, preferring them above ourselves, and yet take measures to protect ourselves and those we love from physical or financial harm?

Yes it is possible. Sometimes there are boundaries that must be drawn. We often need to draw lines. However this must be done with wisdom, patience, humility and love. *It cannot be based on feelings.* And yes, learning to draw lines is a process.

To draw boundaries in relationships, a believer must first know Christ is his/her life, power and identity, and his/her needs of acceptance and security are met in Him only. Then the individual chooses to let go of his self-life–his fleshly strategies and reactions–as he focuses on the mind of Christ being lived out in relation to another.....*as a line is drawn*. Some examples of drawing a line are below, even though we may not be accustomed to thinking of these as boundaries. Remember *we can only draw boundaries for ourselves,* **not others**.

* When one is being *taken advantage of by criminal activity*, the response is to *take whatever legal steps that are necessary*, while keeping the attitude of love and humility.

* If *faced with verbal threats*, the person *with argumentative or dominant flesh–as well as other individuals–*must relinquish the desire to return a threat with a threat. The person must be willing to *lose the prid*e of having to "be right" and quit trying to win or prove he/she is best, even though he/she may look wrong. This person must allow himself or herself to be humbled and know God will exalt him/her in due time. *In doing so, he/she draws a line, ceasing to be hooked into destructive interactions.*

* When someone is constantly *being gossiped about* by another person, he/she needs to remove him/herself from the gossiper. We are *not to associate with a gossip.* Proverbs 20:19 This is drawing a proper boundary. If a believer *sins* **against us,** we should go to them privately and address it with the attitude of Christ. Matthew 18:15 But we should not continue trying to confront, change, or appease the person who continually puts

others down, is negative or inappropriate. At the same time, we must be humble and loving toward them. We are not to receive put-downs and demeaning comments into our hearts – rather only believe truth based on who we are in Christ.

* Anyone who is *falsely accused, rejected, insulted, taken advantage of, gossiped about*, etc. *must forgive. Forgiveness draws a boundary in that it releases the accused from being controlled by the accuser.* The accused needs to let go of harboring anger, hate, revenge–and being defensive. He/she must respond with kindness gentleness, not returning insult for insult, but returning a blessing to those who insult. Sometimes a counselor may be needed to encourage one in this. If there is ongoing **abuse,** one might *need to separate from the abuser.*

Romans 12:19-21 says " Never take your own revenge, beloved, but leave room for the wrath of God, for it is written, "Vengence is mine. I shall re-pay." says the Lord. "But if your enemy is hungry, feed him, and if he is thirsty, give him a drink. And do not be overcome with evil, but overcome evil with good." Do these things even if another's behavior must be confronted or if there must be legal accountability.

* The person with a *victim mind-set* must catch himself when he ruminates on, or consistently verbalizes, how he has been *unfairly treated.* He, as other individuals, must refrain from expecting or forcing others to change. He must accept responsibility in Christ for his thoughts, feelings and actions and *let go of blaming others for them. In doing so he draws a boundary for himself.* He must forgive, remembering that healing and protection are to be found only in the Lord.

* Those of us who are (or *feel* we are) **being dealt with unjustly**, have to know the attitude of Christ *is giving, not getting, and not being "catered- to"*.

* Many people learn early in life to make *assumptions* about what others say and do. They aren't clear and direct in their own communication and believe others also *insinuate*. So they *interpret*, but *they are often wrong*. This can lead to intense conflict. They fear what others think and fear people who are direct. These individuals can, and should, *draw a boundary for themselves by choosing to rest in their identity in Christ and stop interpreting actions and words as rejection.* They must learn to give, serve and build up others in the truth, demanding nothing in return even if there *is* real rejection.

* Another person might *draw a line by saying "no" when appropriate.* When one feels he is being taken advantage by others asking too much of him, he may need to *lay aside his "people-pleasing" manipulation* and doing external behaviors that look like Godly service, but which require appreciation or reward. This person may have to be willing to risk rejection or looking "less-than" as he/she says, "no" and chooses Christ's kind, gentle, patient, and considerate mind-set. This Godly transformation takes time and involves a learning process. One must choose to walk forward in the trial and learn, regardless of negative emotions. The person must serve with the attitude of Christ and stop trying to validate their worth by fleshly service to others. She/he must remind herself/himself that completeness and approval is already hers/his in Christ and not found in another person or situation.

Is There A Line?

* *Wisely* serving others and preferring them above ourselves, **does not mean we must do everything others ask or demand.** We should encourage others to meet their obligations and be accountable. We are not to try to "fix" others and do more for them than they do for themselves. In other words, we are *not to enable* others to be irresponsible by our giving and serving them!

Whether we must draw a boundary or not, we are not to "return evil **for** evil, or **insult for insult**; but, on the contrary, (return) a blessing, because to this you were called, **that you might inherit a blessing.**" 1 Peter 3:9

The vexation of a fool is known at once, but the prudent **ignores an insult.** Pr. 12:16 ESV

Whoever would foster love **covers over an offense**, but whoever repeats the matter separates close friends. Proverbs 17:9 ESV

A person's wisdom yields patience; it is to one's glory to **overlook an offense.** Proverbs 19:11 ESV

16

Do We Often Create Our Hard Times?

Today, I saw this on Facebook, "**Don't Believe Everything You Think.**" I might add, "..especially if what you think is according to the world system."

Our natural, fleshly way of thinking is an expression of the wisdom of the world system. The wisdom of the world, or fleshly wisdom, is thinking and reasoning based on the lusts of the eyes, the lusts of the flesh, and the boastful pride of life. 1 John 2:16 (But it can *seem* so good and right.)

The wisdom of the world is: **all about *me***. What I can accomplish. How I can find significance. What I deserve. My rights. What others should do for me. What is fair. What is not fair. What I can get. How to satisfy my neediness. How to fill my loneliness. How to protect myself. How I can control my life to be secure. How others see me. Even…what I can do for God. It is opposite of Christ's mind-set and thinking in the Kingdom of God. It is an enigma; that Paradox. And the wisdom of this world is foolishness to God. 1 Corinthians 3:19 And God's truth is foolishness to the world. 1 Corinthians 1:18 (KJV)

Christians are a fragrance of Christ to God among those who are being saved *also* among those who are perishing *(the world)*; to the one *(the world)* an aroma from death to death, to the other *(Christians)* an aroma from life to life. 2 Corinthians 2:15-16 The Truth seems like the stench of death to those who hate truth.

The world's way of thinking *can* sound good and even sacrificial. And perhaps religious. Reasoning from worldly wisdom can make a lot of sense. It is a way that can *seem RIGHT,* and it indeed may be influenced by religious principles. But it is deceptive. And following after that way is the way of death. Proverbs 14:12 (The word *death* meaning separation from knowing God and His best for us as communicated in this book.) Out of this thinking we often make decisions and plans based on what we hope will happen–what we are 98% sure will happen–thinking we are exercising faith rather than being "practical". Then we get into trouble, because things didn't turn out the way it seemed they would. Circumstances rarely happen as we expect.

No one has to teach us to think from this worldly wisdom. We are born that way. And programmed under it. As noted previously, much of the programming remains in our soul/mind after we are born-again. It can even be created after we are born-again. And it is reinforced by the world…perhaps even by religion. *And* it creates conflict within us–in our emotions and in our relationships. It *creates* trials and adversity, leaving us depressed and confused, asking God, *Why?*

Wisdom of the world system can also be an obsession with what others do wrong. With Ego. With Pride. It leads to our being offended. It leads to greed, and fighting to be recognized. It can lead to our being catered-to. It often leads to a mind-set of entitlement, living as an extension of, and dependent on, other people–or government. It leads to contention, revenge, rejection, accusation, lying, debt, and war. It leads to immorality. It leads to people engaging in exactly what they accuse others of doing–discrimination, intolerance, prejudice. And it can't bring inner peace. The peace the world gives is only a temporary pause of the outward wars that worldly wisdom creates.

So yes, we do often create our hard times.

When we believers live out of our own personal false beliefs, we are walking after the flesh and after the wisdom of the world. And we are not to do it. It is for our own benefit that we are urged in scripture to turn around *by a change of mind*; be transformed by the renewing of our mind and be conformed to the image of Christ.

Unless we are born-again and know the truth of being transformed, we can continue living according to the wisdom of the world. Our fleshly patterns hook with others' fleshly patterns, and we wonder why we are stuck, defeated, discouraged, angry and T.I.R.E.D.

The intention of our Creator and Father God is to *use the very trials that result from the wisdom of the world system as His instruments to bring us into the experience of His Kingdom*, which is *not of* this world system!

Because we know these truths, we are not to resist hard times. We are told to not harden our hearts to receiving adversity and responding correctly to it. Hebrews 3, says if you hear God speak today, don't be stubborn. Don't be stubborn like those who rebelled in the wilderness and didn't enter into rest because of hardening their hearts.

Christ **learned obedience** by the things he suffered (by the trials He faced). Hebrews 5:8 And so do we. Just as Christ, we must also walk through hard times learning to respond in humility and love, in the same manner as He. Our response cannot be according to the world's wisdom, even though we must be wise as serpents, yet harmless as doves. Matthew 10:16 (KJV) And then we, "with unveiled face, beholding as in a mirror the glory of the Lord, are **being transformed into the same image** from glory to glory." 2 Corinthians 3:18

We must guard against believing what the world believes.

One of the world's beliefs is *"emotions represent truth."* But the fact is, how we *feel* is a product of what we *think*. Emotions *follow* what we think. It is surprising how many of us *live life based on how we FEEL*. Today, many people *feel offended*, and they blame it on others. And they try to force others to change for them to *feel* okay.

We hear multiple times a day, "They *made me feel..*" this way or that way. "They offended me." "They *made me angry*." "His treating me unfairly *made me do that*." "*It is her fault* that I hit her." "Because of what she said, she is guilty of causing that riot and people getting hurt. She should be charged with inciting violence"... They blame others for their own *feelings* and even their *behaviors*! They demand that, "Laws must be made so people who are biased and unfair will be prosecuted", not knowing that matters of the heart can not be changed by legislation.

It's the Blame Game. Some people *use* being a victim as an opportunity to get what they want. But it doesn't satisfy. So they do more of the same. And others are so accomplished in blaming that they can instantly turn any blame directed toward them onto another person or situation.

Instead of resisting temptation, people with a worldly mind-set can *blame the object of their temptation* for their response to it! We often think of lust and temptation in a sexual context. But that is only one of many types of lusts.

Individuals often even blame their emotional state *on others* being insensitive! But no one else can *make us feel* or *do* this or that. We are responsible for how we feel and what we do. *Negative or damaging emotions result from worldly wisdom*–one's own false thinking about life and how needs should be met. For our own good, we must stop blaming others for our emotions and behaviors and take responsibility for them. Not taking responsibility for them gives others control over us.

***Feeling* offended is a huge issue.** The word, *offend*, means to trap or bait or cause one to stumble. And scripture tells us to not offend others. But in our society, when one says he/she is offended, it means they feel disrespected, insulted, put-down, or slighted and they believe they are *entitled* to respect.

Feeling offended comes from a mind-set that can include speculating, assuming, and indirect communication. This involves emotions as self-pity, anger, hatred, resentment, revenge, unforgiveness, and jealousy. This can lead to quarrels, theft, deceit, revenge, and abuse. The offended person often vows that he/she *will see to it* that the offender doesn't get away with what he/she did! *Feeling* offended leads to sin.

Although someone may say offensive things, the person who hears those things **chooses** to *feel* offended – **or not**. A certain thing that is said may offend one person and not another. **The person's belief system is behind his/her *feeling* offended.** People who are easily offended have unmet needs that only God can meet.

Think about this. We can offend others by *feeling offended*. The calling of a disciple of Christ is to choose to pass on by when the temptation to take up an offense comes. The call is to forgive, tolerate, understand, show mercy, overlook offenses, and show love and humility to others, including the offender, preferring them over one's self. Love isn't provoked or annoyed to anger or indignation. 1 Corinthians 13:5

Pride, ego and feeling inferior are most often behind *feeling* offended. In putting on humility, a believer needs to accept his/her identity in Christ and then let go of the pride of life and things being *all about me*, as he/she puts on the mind of Christ. It is the cure for *feeling* offended. The world's wisdom is about ego–my importance, my possessions, my comfort, my fun, my rights, and my feelings.

There are many ways that pride can cause one to *feel* offended. For example, various types of personal strife and conflict grow from pride. Someone's preference of another instead of me can lead to envy. This is the very reason God calls believers to be conformed to the image of Christ. We can then enter into and partake of the freedom that is our inheritance in Him.

We can be so *sensory*, living by our five senses, rather than by truth and the spirit. Humility and the *agape'* love to which we refer here is not living by our senses, our attractions, nor by our affections. (However *phileo* love, or brotherly affection, is good and necessary among the body of Christ as it arises from Truth.)

Most people who are easily *offended* feel rejected, insecure, overly sensitive and are threated by a lot of things. They can be critical and negative. We often hear them saying, "I went there and hardly anyone spoke to me." (I wonder how many *he* spoke to...) Or, " He was curt with me. I won't tolerate that. I'll put him in his place." Or, "She was insinuating.... thus and so...."

Feeling offended can lead to quarrels. We aren't to live in conflict, being contentious, which is being argumentative, quarrelsome, disagreeable. But are to refuse foolish and ignorant speculations, (assumptions) knowing they produce quarrels. The Lord's bond-servant must not be quarrelsome, but be kind to all, able to teach, patient when wronged." 2 Timothy 2:23-24 We are to destroy our speculations by taking every thought captive to the obedience of Christ.

2 Corinthians 10:5

A lot of us are direct and to the point, and that often *offends* others who insinuate and are indirect, and who learned early in life to *speculate and interpret* what they think others mean. This leads to suspicion, confusion and quarrels. They don't know the Word tells us to cast down speculations.

It seems that we *expect* to be *offended*. And here I'm giving actual examples of comments from believers in the church. Not too long ago, Angie asked Max "What are you doing?" Max retorted, "Why do you want to know what I am doing? What did you mean by that?" His perception was there was something hidden in her question. Some might say that Angie's past attitudes have *made* Max this way. Max *felt offended*, and Angie was blamed.

Comments that are gestures of love to the person saying them, can be taken as put-downs by the other! This happens a lot. Meme's expression of love to her son was, "The forecast says there will be icy roads in the morning, so do be careful." Her son told a friend, "My Mom thinks I am stupid and can't take care of myself!" He felt *offended*.

Even a small suggestion to another many times can be received as demeaning! Roscoe and Sylvia were hanging out on their vacation. She was holding a camera, and he noticed a beautiful scene with just the right shadows. He said, "That is great. Go over and get a picture of that!" It was the usual way he makes suggestions. Instantly Sylvia began sulking...she thought he was trying to control her. And she was *offended*. In her worldly thinking, telling her what to do makes her "less-than". The fact is that even though Sylvia is a nice person, *she* is known for being controlling!

Many hard times happen because we believe we should put our trust in other people as well in ourselves. God, knowing humans can not supply our needs and fill our longings, commanded we love and trust Him and His grace for those benefits. *His grace frees us from the expectations we put on ourselves and on others.*

The previous comments illustrate ways we can create our own hard times. But in life hard times come regardless. Scripture calls them adversities, trials, afflictions, tribulations. In Hebrew the word, *tribulation,* means a pressing together, like a squeezing or pinching – which we all have experienced. Trials can be big and firey, or not. They might be smaller situations–thorns that prick or goad us. Or smoldering embers that could turn into a raging fire. *Regardless, the Lord uses them as opportunities for us to grow up into His best.*

Born again believers have been set free by Christ's sacrifice. By His life in us, we can decide to walk in His wisdom, freedom, power and blessings in response to the hard times.

We must learn to make decisions in life based on *Godly wisdom,* which is making choices *based on knowledge of His truth*, and being *prudent. Prudent* means being *practical and frugal.* Along with these, we need to *use discretion*, which means being *cautious, careful and prudent* based on God's Word. Proverbs 8:12

We might have thought we used Godly wisdom in making plans that didn't turn out as we expected. But walking after our own understanding and the wisdom of the world and the subtle deceptions of Satan leads to confusion, discouragement, fatigue,

Do We Often Create Our Hard Times?

and/or to other dire consequences. The good news is the Lord uses even the trials that may result from our decisions to bring us into His best – if we respond correctly to them.

Jesus said, behold, I have given you authority to tread on serpents and scorpions, and **over all the power of the enemy**, and nothing will injure you. Luke 10:19 And exercising that power is living the *Paradox*.

17

In Summary

Responding correctly to trials, hard times and adversity, removes blocks and hindrances to believers experiencing the fullness of Christ and the blessings that are already theirs as new creations in Him. These responses are choices we make by the power of Christ who dwells in us. They involve an inner discipline–our obedience of faith and God's will for us.

When responding to trials & adversity:

1. First, we must have believed God's grace and that we have been unconditionally accepted by Him. We must know we are one with Christ, forgiven of all our sins, righteous in Him and have been made **new creations with His life and power indwelling us.** We must *know our identity* in Christ. We need to know God is our provision and protection. Psalm 18:1-3, Philippians 4:19

2. We are to *not be surprised* **by the fiery ordeal as if some strange thing is happening to us.** Rather we need to be ready and watchful, knowing the testing WILL come. 1 Peter 4: 12-17

3. **We are to *arm ourselves with the mind of Christ*** – humility, love, forgiveness, sacrifice and the heart of a servant, as we *die to* or *relinquish* self-protective, self-promoting ways. This is our armor of protection. To do this, we must be in the Word and know the truth.
   1 Peter 4, Philippians 2:5-8, Romans 12:2 (The full armor is in Ephesians 6:13-17)
4. **Resolve to *receive the trial* when it comes**, and to replace our old mind-set with the same attitude as Christ, which is our taking every thought captive to the obedience of Christ. 2 Corinthians 10:5
5. **Do *not be ashamed*** if you are a believer and undergoing pain. There is a reason for it. 1 Peter 4:16
6. ***Rejoice in the Lord*** through the hard time. It will not last forever. Don't be discouraged. Keep reminding yourself it is for God's purpose to work His will – the mind of Christ–in you. Peter 4:13, James 1:2
7. **We must *persevere through the trial*.** . For you have need of **endurance,** so that *when you have done this will of God, you may partake of the reward.* Hebrews 10:35-36
8. ***Be careful to not take up offenses.*** 2 Timothy 2:23-24 **Guard against believing what the world believes.** 1 Corinthians 3:19 Be wise in 'drawing a line'. Do not create your own hard times.

As a result of making the above choices:

1. When we humble ourselves, putting on the mind of Christ, **it is offering up *spiritual sacrifices*.** 1 Peter 2:5
2. The life of **Jesus will be revealed** or *manifest* **in our *mortal* flesh** (body). 2 Corinthians 4: 8-11

In Summary

3. We **grow up in Him** and are **transformed by the renewing of our mind,** being **conformed to the image of Christ,** proving what the **will of God is**–that which is good, acceptable and perfect. Ephesians 4:15, Romans 12:2
4. We **take hold of** (*experience*) **eternal life and know God.** John 17:3 We partake more fully of our inheritance–the **kingdom of Heaven** that is within–His rest, righteousness, abundant joy and peace–in our daily walk. Romans 14:17, 1 Timothy 6: 12,19 We will *receive the reward of the inheritance.* Colossians 3: 3,24
5. Those who remain steadfast, after they have suffered a while, He will *mature, establish, strengthen and settle.* 1 Peter 5:9-10
6. We will be *perfect* (mature) *and complete, lacking in nothing,* James 1:2-4 and **share His holiness.** Hebrews 12:10-11
7. Others will **see Christ in and through us, and they will glorify God,** because in seeing / experiencing Him **they are lead to repentance.** Romans 2:4 *This is when we let our light shine.* Matthew 5:16
8. We will be **known as His disciples.** John 13:35,
9. We will **receive the crown of life.** James 1:12
10. **Endurance** will have been produced in us. James 1:2
11. We will experience the **salvation** (deliverance) **of our soul,** (our mind, emotions). 1 Peter 1:7-11
12. His peace will **guard our hearts and minds.** Philippian 4:7

So be encouraged in knowing:

*   In order to know Christ in the power of His resurrection as we live in this world, we must also **know Him in the fellowship of His sufferings, being conformed to His death.** Philippians

3:10 To know Christ in the power of His resurrection is to lay hold on and walk in His power, fulfillment and freedom.

* Jesus said, "If you will follow me, **you must take up your cross and deny yourselves.**" Matthew 16:24 One's "cross" is the trial that is perfectly suited to break one's reliance on fleshly strategies. Watchman Nee said that the Lord "wants to break our outward man in order that the inward man (*Christ*) may have a way out."

* Jesus said that **whosoever *doesn't take up His cross, cannot be His disciple.*** Luke 14:26, 27

* A trial provides **the opportunity** for one's *response* to it (one's attitude or mind-set) **to be Christ's likeness** – His image. Philippians 2:5-8 It is God's will for us. Romans 12:2, 8:2

* All **who would be Godly will be persecuted.** II Timothy 3:12 It is for the purpose of bringing out God's holiness.

* It is **through many tribulations** we must enter *(experience)* the Kingdom of God. Acts 14:22 Entering the Kingdom of God is *experiencing* in our daily life the righteousness, peace and joy in the Holy Spirit *that is already ours in Christ.*

* And not only this, but we also **exult in our tribulations** knowing tribulation brings about **perseverance**, and perseverance, proven **character**, and proven character, **hope**.... Romans 5: 3-5

* **Blessed are you** when men hate you, and ostracize you, and **insult** you, and scorn your name as evil, **for** the sake of the Son of Man. Luke 6:22

* Therefore I am well content with **weaknesses, with insults, with distresses, with persecutions, with difficulties, for** Christ's sake; **for** when I am weak, then I am strong. 2 Corinthians 12:10

In Summary

* In our not returning evil **for** evil or **insult for insult**, but giving a blessing instead; **for** you were called **for** the very purpose that you might **inherit a blessing.** 1 Peter 3:9
* We are to **take His yoke** of humility and learn of Him. Matthew 11:29
* He disciplines us so we would **share his holiness.** Heb. 12:10
* For **to you it has been granted** for Christ's sake, not only to believe in Him, but also **to suffer for His sake.** Philippians 1:29
* **Blessed is the man who perseveres** (remains steadfast) **under trial,** for when he has been approved (stood the test) he will receive **the crown of life**, which God has promised to those who love him. James 1:12
* **Many are the afflictions of the righteous**, But the Lord **delivers him** out of them all. Psalm 34:19 You will walk through the fire and will not be burned. Isaiah 43:2
* **I am well content** with weaknesses, with insults with distresses, with persecutions, with difficulties, for Christ's sake; for when I am weak, then I am strong. 2 Corinthians 12:10

Just as Jesus learned obedience by the things He suffered, so we also learn our obedience of faith in hard times and trials. And we must know it is **by the life and power of Christ within that we choose these inner changes of mind and heart.**

We who identify ourselves as *believers* often see the Christian life as behavior modification and/or as a life *focused on* what God will give and what He will do for us. In connection, there is the expectation that He will remove the hard times in our lives. But the purpose of this book has been to reveal another perspective regarding God's will for us which is, in receiving the difficulties of life with correct responses, we *will know Him, His life will be revealed through us*, and we will *experience* the awesome blessings, that by His grace, are already ours in Christ.

It is evident that God's will is **woven into and worked out of** adversities and trials in the lives of His people. A **divine design.**

Finally, be strong in the Lord and in the strength of His might. Put on the full armor of God, so that you will be able to stand firm against the schemes of the devil. For our struggle in trials is not against flesh and blood, but against the rulers, against the powers, against the world forces of this darkness, against the spiritual forces of wickedness in the heavenly places. ... Ephesians 6:10-18

It is by God's grace, forgiveness, and His indwelling presence that we derive power to walk in Christ's likeness and thus live in His best. However, some believe that since they are unconditionally accepted and forgiven by His grace, they can do whatever they *feel* like doing. And they don't understand why they suffer the consequences. God's freedom, grace, protection and power are ours inwardly and outwardly so we can we choose to love and fulfill our calling. It is so we can walk in the freedom for which He set us free, rather than receiving His grace in vain.

When we respond in our hard times by Christ's likeness, we "will go out with joy and be led forth with peace; The mountains and the hills will break forth into shouts of joy before you, and all of the trees of the field will clap their hands." Isaiah 55:12

Appendix

A Biblical Picture of Mankind:

Mankind: A Three-Part Whole I Thessalonians 5:23, Hebrews 4:12

Body, Soul & Spirit

A person *In Adam* walking *In the Flesh* Romans. 8:8

The gray areas depict "original sin", spiritual death, and independence from God (Flesh) in a person before he is born-again. The power of sin drives this person as he lives in his environment, to draw conclusions (False Beliefs) about God, self, and how needs are to be met, which are stored in the soul and lived out through the body. The resulting outer actions can look good OR bad. **And death separates the person from knowing God. One's identity is SINNER. Rom. 5:8**

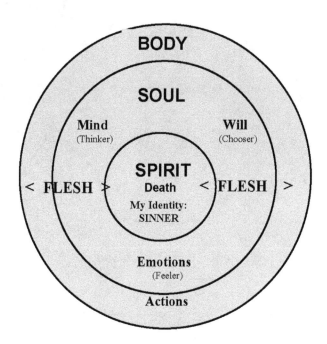

A New Creation In Christ: 2 Cor. 5:17

A Person *In the Spirit* but walking *After the Flesh* Rom. 8:9
This shows a person whose dead spirit has been replaced with Christ's Spirit and Life. This person has been born again of the Spirit. **Christ is now the person's identity and power, but the person is not yet walking after the Spirit, but after the flesh.** The fleshly patterns block our experience of Christ's life in us.

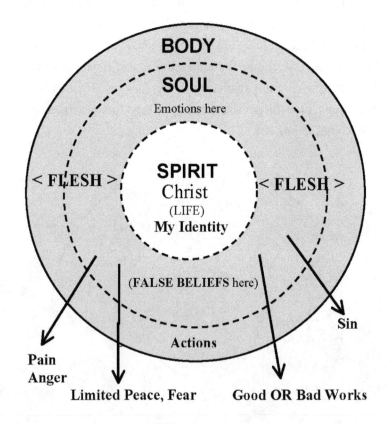

A human is a _____ who has a _____ and lives in a _____.

A Biblical Picture of Mankind:

New Creation - Walking After the Spirit:

The diagram below might be a helpful aid in understanding the truth of how the gray areas of flesh are being broken by the adversities of daily life.

(One's dependency on flesh is being "broken". Christ's life is flowing out.)

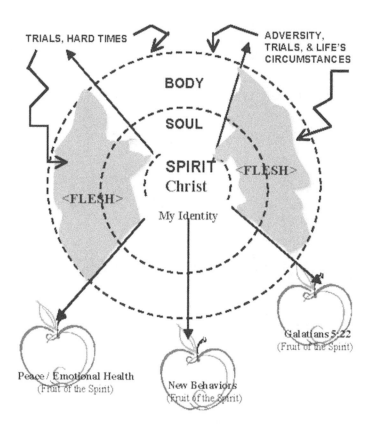

This is when we choose to be **transformed by the renewing of our mind** and **conformed to the image of Christ**. It is to **mature in Him** & **pursue holiness**.

Some Examples of False Beliefs vs Truth

Use the following table to identify some of your False Beliefs about how longings and needs of Security, Worth and Peace are to be met. It may help you to be aware of any unconscious beliefs you have. Focus on replacing them with truth. A more extensive table can be found in my book, *Old Beliefs vs New Beliefs*.

False Beliefs vs Truth

False Beliefs	Truth
1. I must control circumstances for me (and my family) to be **secure**.	I am secure because I am hidden with Christ in God. Col.3:3. All my needs are supplied in Christ. Phil. 4: 19 It is not by my power nor strength, but by His Spirit. Zech.4:6 He is a shield to those who walk uprightly. Pr. 2:7b
2. I must perform perfectly and avoid mistakes to be **acceptable**.	I am perfect in Christ; one spirit with Him. Heb.10:14; I Cor. 6:17 I have been made accepted by Him. Eph.1:6 Christ died that I would be the righteousness of God in Him. I Cor. 5:21
3. I must stay emotionally guarded to be safe and **secure**.	The Lord is my safety. Ps. 4:8; 27:1-6; 32: 7-11 Safety is only of the Lord. Pr. 1:33; 3:23; 21:31 As I trust Christ, His peace will guard my heart and mind. Phil.4:7 He is my shield and fortress. Ps. 18:1-3

4. I must be strong and independent to **survive.**	Christ's strength is perfect in my weakness. II Cor.12: 9 My life is to be dependent on Christ, since He is the Vine and I am a branch in Him. Without Him I can do <u>nothing</u>. John 15:5; II Cor.12:10
5. I am entitled to get respect from, and be appreciated by, others to know I am **of worth** and not rejected.	I am called to love, and to serve others and consider them better than myself. Phil. 2:3 Pride comes before destruction and shame. Pr.16:18; 11:2 I am to become of "no reputation" and be a servant. Phil. 2:5-8. Christ has made me accepted and perfect. Eph.1: 6; Heb.10:14 See #2
6. I need others to accept me and treat me fairly so I can find **peace.**	Jesus Christ is my peace and gives me peace. John 14:27. I am in perfect peace when my mind is fixed on Him. As I humble myself, I will enjoy peace. Ps. 37:11, Is. 26:3
7. What I do makes me **who I am.**	Birth determines my identity. I have been made a new creation by my new birth. The old me died with Christ. Gal. 2: 20; II Cor. 5: 17
8. I am **inadequate.** I must please others to know I am **acceptable.**	I have been made adequate. 2 Cor.3:5-6 I can do all things through Christ. I am complete in Him. Col.2:10; Phil.4:13 He makes me adequate to do His will. Heb.13:21 See #9

Some Examples of False Beliefs vs Truth

9. I must prove I am right to know I am **of worth**.	Christ has made me accepted in Him. Eph.1: 6; Ps.139, 13-18 I am chosen, righteous, holy, a saint: A new creation. II Cor.5:17; I Peter 2: 9; I Cor.1: 2 See #2, #5
10. People from my past must change (admit their offenses against me, etc.) before I can be free of my childhood issues and **be O.K**	My issues *have* been dealt with because I have died with Christ and am a new creation. I am O.K. when I accept that He has given me the victory. I can cease from my struggling. Heb.4:10

My True Identity In Christ

By God's unconditional Love, Mercy and Grace, as a born-again believer, my old dead spirit of sin has been exchanged for Christ's Spirit in me. The following is who I am as a new creation in my spirit person.

Matt. 5:13	I am the salt of the earth.
Matt 5:14	I am the Light of the world.
John 1:12	I am a child of God (part of His family).
John 15:15	I am part of the True Vine, (a branch) of Christ's life.
Rom. 6:18	I have been freed from the bondage of sin.
Rom. 8:16	I am a child of God
Rom. 8:17	I am a joint-heir with Christ, sharing His inheritance
I Cor. 3:16,	I am a temple (house) of God. His Spirit (His life) dwells in me. 1 Cor. 6:19
I Cor. 6:17	I am joined to the Lord and am one spirit with Him.
I Cor.12:27	I am a member (part) of Christ's body (Eph. 5:30).
II Cor. 5:17	I am a new creation, holy, perfect, righteous in Christ.
Gal. 3:26	I am a son of God and one with Christ.
Eph. 1:1	I am a saint (see I Cor. 1:2 Phil. 1: 1Col. 1:2).
Eph. 2:10	I am God's workmanship created (born anew) in Christ.
Eph. 4:24	I am righteous and holy.
Col. 3:3	I am hidden with Christ in God.
Col. 3:12	I am chosen of God, holy, and dearly loved.
I Thess. 5:5	I am a son of light and not of darkness.

Adapted from materials by GMI, and used by permission.
From Old Beliefs vs New Beliefs © 2015, Anne Trippe

Painful Messages and Beliefs

Sometimes *traumatic circumstances* happen in our lives, especially in our formative years. Pain, rejection, loss, abuse, or even being "catered-to", can result in false messages (false beliefs) about ourselves, about how to stay safe, and about how other needs are to be met. And the messages *may* be outside of our awareness. But it is out of them that we develop ineffective ways of living in relationships. We sometimes avoid, fight, give in, or fill our emptiness in other ways. We might live with anger, hopelessness, fear, or depression .

If there has been a certain hurtful situation in our life that we can't get past, it is good to *acknowledge to ourselves the person and situation, and identify our false beliefs or hurtful messages that are associated with that person. We should be aware of the power the messages have had over us.*

We need to begin receiving God's love, His healing, and our true identity in Christ in order to *renounce those old messages*. Renouncing means to consciously walk away from false messages, past rejections, fears and pain **as we focus on truth** of God's love and our true identity in Him.

Our **forgiving others** (cancelling the debt) is part of this turning to truth and a necessary part of our experiencing healing and our freedom in Christ. Forgiveness is not saying the other's actions were not wrong. Forgiveness doesn't mean we need to have a close relationship with the offender. And it may take a while for our feelings to line up with truth.

Sometimes we might need another person, maybe a counselor in the body of Christ, to come beside us, encourage us, listen to us, and pray with us as we identify, renounce, and receive healing from the past hurts, which can involve feelings of shame, fear, inferiority, or even traits of narcissism.

Our messages/beliefs and resulting behaviors determine how we respond to, trials and adversity.

VIP: If there are suicidal thoughts, there may be medical or physical causes which must be assessed.

A Brief Review

Points to remember when choosing to face trials & hard times

Christ's life and faith indwells the spirit of a believer and is the power by which the believer chooses in the face of adversity to grow, *experience* Christ's life, and be known as His disciple. The following is involved in choosing to set one's mind on things above.

* It is to believe and set one's mind on God's grace, forgiveness and promises.
* It is to know truths of one's unconditional acceptance and identity as a new creation in Christ.
* It *is not* by efforts to put away old thinking and patterns.
* It is like setting one's mind on learning a new language. It is to focus on choosing Christ's humility and attitude – (one's armor).
* It is to relax and cease one's struggle or striving to satisfy neediness by self-reliance and self-effort. Ps. 46:10, Heb. 10:4
* It isn't passivity or based on emotions. It is an inner discipline, in which one must exercise daily.
* It is to abide (continue or persevere) in the above. It is ongoing. John 15:4,5,10
* It is yielding one's will and ways of trying to control life to God.
* Sometimes one may temporarily *feel* embarrassed, humiliated, rejected, overlooked, or fearful when walking through a trial.
* It is one's obedience of faith. Romans 16:26, 1:5

Fulfilling our calling by living after the Spirit

Facing life with the mind or attitude of Christ **is our calling as believers.**

Philippians 3:13-15 (KJV)
13 Brethren, I count not myself to have apprehended: but this one thing I do, forgetting those things which are behind, and reaching forth unto those things which are before, 14 I press toward the mark for the prize of **the high calling** of God in Christ Jesus. 15 Let us therefore, as many as be perfect, *(mature)* **be thus minded:** and if in any thing ye be otherwise minded, God shall reveal even this unto you.

Ephesians 4:1-3
4 Therefore I, the prisoner of the Lord, implore you to walk in a manner **worthy of the calling** with which you have been called, 2 with **all humility and gentleness, with patience, showing tolerance for one another in love,** 3 being diligent to preserve the unity of the Spirit in the bond of peace.

Ephesians 1:17-19
17 that the God of our Lord Jesus Christ, the Father of glory, may give to you a spirit of wisdom and of revelation in the knowledge of Him. 18 I pray that the eyes of your heart may be enlightened, so that **you will know what is the hope of His calling, what are the riches of the glory of His inheritance** in the saints, 19 and what is the surpassing **greatness of His power toward us who believe. These are in accordance with the working of the strength of His might.**

Ephesians 2:10

⁰For we are His workmanship, created in Christ Jesus for good works, which God prepared beforehand so that we would walk in them.

Colossians 3:3-4

For **you have died and your life is hidden with Christ in God.** ⁴ **When Christ,** *who is our life,* *is revealed,* then you also will be revealed with Him in **(His)** glory.

Mainstay Scriptures

Psalm 91

He who dwells in the shelter of the Most High
Will abide in the shadow of the Almighty.
²I will say to the LORD, "My refuge and my fortress,
My God, in whom I trust!"
³For it is He who delivers you from the snare of the trapper
And from the deadly pestilence.
⁴He will cover you with His pinions,
And under His wings you may seek refuge;
His faithfulness is a shield and bulwark.

⁵You will not be afraid of the terror by night,
Or of the arrow that flies by day;
⁶Of the pestilence that stalks in darkness,
Or of the destruction that lays waste at noon.
⁷A thousand may fall at your side
And ten thousand at your right hand,
But it shall not approach you.
⁸You will only look on with your eyes
And see the recompense of the wicked.
⁹For you have made the LORD, my refuge,
Even the Most High, your dwelling place.
¹⁰No evil will befall you,
Nor will any plague come near your [c]tent.

continued

[11] For He will give His angels charge concerning you,
To guard you in all your ways.
[12] They will bear you up in their hands,
That you do not strike your foot against a stone.
[13] You will tread upon the lion and cobra,
The young lion and the serpent you will trample down.
[14] "Because he has loved Me, therefore I will deliver him;
I will set him *securely* on high, because he has known My name.
[15] "He will call upon Me, and I will answer him;
I will be with him in trouble;
I will rescue him and honor him.
[16] "With a long life I will satisfy him
And let him see My salvation."

Isaiah 40:31

Yet those who wait for the Lord
Will gain new strength;
They will mount up *with* wings like eagles,
They will run and not get tired,
They will walk and not become weary.

Psalm 46:10

"**Cease *striving*** and know that I am God; I will be exalted among the nations, I will be exalted in the earth."

CPSIA information can be obtained
at www.ICGtesting.com
Printed in the USA
LVHW010233040519
616662LV00027B/354/P